Optimizing Real-Time Analytics

Ibrahim Olushola

© 2024 Ibrahim Olushola

All rights reserved.

No part of this book, *OPTIMIZING REAL TIME ANALYTICS*", may be reproduced, distributed, or transmitted in any form or by any means, including photocopying, recording, or other electronic or mechanical methods, without the prior written permission of the author, except in the case of brief quotations embodied in critical reviews and certain other noncommercial uses permitted by copyright law

TABLE OF CONTENTS

chapter 1	1
The Foundations of Real-Time Analytics	
Chapter 2	8
Understanding Real-Time Data Pipelines	
Chapter 3	16
The Role of Cloud Computing in Real-Time Analytics	
Chapter 4	26
Real-Time Analytics Use Cases Across Industries	
Chapter 5	36
Building High-Performance Real-Time Systems	
Chapter 6	46
Real-Time Visualization and Reporting	
Chapter 7	58
Security and Privacy in Real-Time Analytics	
Chapter 8	69
Integrating Machine Learning in Real-Time Analytics	
Chapter 9	77
Measuring and Maximizing the ROI of Real Time Analytics	
Chapter 10	85
Envisioning the Future of Real-Time Analytics	

Preface	iv
Foreword	vi
Introduction	viii

PREFACE

In today's fast-paced, interconnected world, the ability to make decisions based on real-time data is no longer a luxury reserved for the tech elite, it has become an essential tool for survival and success in nearly every industry. From finance to healthcare, retail to transportation, and everything in between, real-time analytics has emerged as the cornerstone of innovation, operational efficiency, and adaptability. This dynamic field empowers organizations to stay ahead of the curve, respond to changes as they happen, and predict outcomes with a level of precision that was once unimaginable. Yet, despite its transformative potential, the full power of real-time analytics remains untapped in many areas, constrained by technical complexities, lack of strategic implementation, or an underestimation of its capabilities. This book is my effort to bridge that gap, offering readers a comprehensive guide to understanding, implementing, and maximizing the profound impact of real-time analytics.

In writing *Optimizing Real-Time Analytics*, I drew deeply from my own journey of working with data-driven systems and witnessing firsthand how real-time insights have revolutionized operations, decision-making, and innovation across industries. Over the years, I have seen organizations transform their processes, gain competitive advantages, and improve the lives of their customers, all by leveraging the actionable insights that real-time analytics provides. But I have also observed missed opportunities, where the potential of real-time data went unrealized due to a lack of understanding or proper tools. This book, therefore, is not merely a technical manual; it is a roadmap for harnessing the power of real-time analytics to solve real-world problems, empower teams, and deliver tangible results.

My vision for this book is to make it accessible and valuable to a diverse audience. Whether you are a seasoned data scientist, a business executive navigating the complexities of digital transformation, or a technology enthusiast curious about the future of data, this book has something for you. The principles, strategies, and examples shared here are designed to

INTRODUCTION

The digital age has brought with it an explosion of data more than we ever imagined possible. Every click we make online, every transaction we complete in stores, every device we use, and even the infrastructure around us constantly generates streams of data. This unprecedented scale and speed of data generation present both an incredible opportunity and a significant challenge. While the sheer volume of data might seem overwhelming, the true power of data lies not in its collection but in the insights it can provide. Nowhere is this potential more apparent or impactful than in the realm of real-time analytics.

Real-time analytics is the process of collecting, processing, and analyzing data as it happens. Unlike traditional analytics, which primarily examines historical data, real-time systems empower organizations to respond to events as they unfold. This capability introduces a new level of agility, enabling businesses and institutions to seize opportunities, mitigate risks, and make informed decisions at the moment they are needed. Whether it's a retail company using real-time data to optimize product recommendations for individual customers, a financial institution detecting fraudulent activity before it causes damage, or healthcare provider monitoring patient vitals to prevent medical emergencies, real-time analytics is reshaping industries and redefining what is possible in an increasingly data-driven world.

The implications of real-time analytics are vast and profound. It is more than just a technological advancement, it is a fundamental shift in how we approach decision-making, problem-solving, and innovation. The ability to act on live data has become a critical differentiator for organizations seeking to maintain a competitive edge in today's rapidly evolving landscape. From enhancing customer experiences to improving operational efficiency and enabling predictive capabilities, the impact of real-time analytics is being felt across every sector.

retail, the examples in this book illuminate how real-time analytics is reshaping industries and solving some of today's most pressing challenges. Ibrahim also addresses the nuances that are often overlooked, such as the ethical implications of data use, the importance of scalability, and the need for a resilient and adaptable infrastructure.

What I find particularly compelling about this book is its forward-looking perspective. Real-time analytics is not static; it is evolving rapidly alongside advancements in artificial intelligence, machine learning, edge computing, and other transformative technologies. Ibrahim dedicates significant attention to these emerging trends, providing readers with a vision of where the field is headed and how they can position themselves or their organizations to stay ahead of the curve. His insights into the future of real-time analytics are both inspiring and thought-provoking, challenging readers to think creatively about the possibilities that lie ahead.

It is rare to find a book that so effectively bridges the gap between theory and practice, offering both a robust technical foundation and actionable strategies for implementation. Ibrahim has provided us with a blueprint for navigating the complexities of real-time analytics, one that is grounded in practical experience and enriched by a deep understanding of its broader implications. The guidance contained within these pages is not only valuable but also empowering, equipping readers to tackle challenges, seize opportunities, and drive meaningful change in their respective fields.

I am confident that *Optimizing Real-Time Analytics* will become an essential resource for anyone looking to harness the power of real-time insights. Whether you are embarking on your journey into this field or seeking to refine and expand your existing capabilities, this book will serve as a trusted guide. Ibrahim's thoughtful and comprehensive approach ensures that readers leave with not only knowledge but also the confidence to apply it effectively. I encourage you to dive into this book with curiosity and an open mind, you will undoubtedly find it as enlightening and empowering as I did.

FOREWORD

The pace of change in today's digital economy is nothing extraordinary, and the driving force behind this transformation is data. From startups to multinational corporations, from local governments to international organizations, the reliance on data to inform decisions, optimize processes, and innovation has become ubiquitous. At the heart of this data revolution lies real-time analytics, the ability to process and analyze data as it is generated, providing actionable insights in the moment. This capability is no longer a competitive advantage reserved for the elite few; it has become a fundamental necessity for those who want to thrive in an increasingly fast-paced and interconnected world. Yet, despite its growing importance, real-time analytics remains a complex and challenging field. It demands not only technical proficiency but also strategic insight to unlock its full potential. That is why this book, *Optimizing Real-Time Analytics*, arrives at such a critical juncture.

Ibrahim Olushola has masterfully distilled his wealth of expertise into this comprehensive guide. With years of experience navigating the intricacies of data systems and strategies, he brings a depth of knowledge that is both impressive and accessible. What sets this book apart is its balance—it caters to readers of diverse backgrounds, whether you are a data scientist eager to deepen your technical skills, a business leader looking to leverage analytics for growth, or a curious professional seeking to understand the mechanics of this transformative field. Ibrahim's writing is clear, practical, and engaging, breaking down complex concepts into digestible insights that resonate with experts and newcomers alike.

One of the standout features of this book is its holistic approach. While many resources on real-time analytics focus narrowly on technical implementation, *Optimizing Real-Time Analytics* goes far beyond the basics. Ibrahim not only lays out the technical foundations explaining architectures, tools, and processes but also delves into the real-world applications that make this field so impactful. From predictive maintenance in manufacturing to personalized customer experiences in equip you with the tools, frameworks, and mindset necessary to unlock the full potential of real-time analytics in your organization or field of interest. Each chapter builds on the last, guiding you through the foundational concepts, advanced techniques, and practical applications of this ever-evolving discipline.

The journey of authoring this book has been both challenging and rewarding, filled with moments of reflection, discovery, and collaboration. It has given me the opportunity to revisit the projects, challenges, and successes that have shaped my understanding of this field. Along the way, I have been fortunate to learn from some of the brightest minds in data science, business strategy, and technology development. I owe a debt of gratitude to the colleagues, mentors, and friends who generously shared their insights, critiques, and encouragement throughout this process. Their contributions have enriched the content and broadened the perspectives presented in this book.

I would also like to extend my heartfelt thanks to you, the reader, for embarking on this journey with me. Your curiosity and commitment to exploring the world of real-time analytics are what make this work meaningful. It is my sincere hope that as you turn the pages of this book, you find not only the knowledge you seek but also the inspiration to explore new horizons, challenge conventional thinking, and push the boundaries of what is possible. Real-time analytics is not just about data; it is about transformation, creativity, and innovation.

The future belongs to those who can harness the power of real-time insights to adapt, anticipate, and thrive in a constantly changing world. As you immerse yourself in the concepts and case studies presented in this book, I encourage you to think boldly and strategically about how real-time analytics can reshape your work, your organization, and your industry. Together, let us unlock the limitless possibilities of real-time analytics and build a future where data-driven intelligence is a force for growth, innovation, and positive change.

This book is designed to provide a comprehensive exploration of real-time analytics, guiding you through its foundational principles, advanced applications, and emerging trends. Divided into ten chapters, it covers everything from the technical architectures that underpin real-time systems to the ethical considerations that must guide their use. We will explore how machine learning enhances real-time analytics, enabling systems to not only process data faster but also learn and improve from it. We will discuss practical strategies for implementing real-time systems effectively and examine the future trends that are poised to reshape the field even further. Along the way, I have included real-world examples, actionable insights, and thought-provoking discussions to help you apply these concepts in your own work and context.

One of the key messages of this book is that real-time analytics is more than just a technical discipline, it is a mindset. It represents a new way of thinking about data and decision-making in the modern world, one that challenges us to be proactive, adaptive, and innovative. Real-time analytics forces us to move beyond reactive approaches to embrace a culture of anticipation and action, where insights are not just descriptive but predictive and prescriptive. It asks us to imagine a world where decisions are guided by the most up-to-date information available, empowering individuals and organizations to act with confidence and precision.

My hope is that this book will inspire you to embrace the transformative possibilities of real-time analytics and equip you with the knowledge, tools, and strategies needed to harness its full potential. Whether you are a data professional looking to deepen your technical expertise, a business leader seeking to drive innovation and improve outcomes, or simply someone curious about the world of analytics, this book is for you. It is designed to be accessible and engaging, offering insights that resonate regardless of your background or level of experience.

The journey ahead is one of discovery and opportunity. Together, we will explore the foundational principles that make real-time analytics possible, delve into its applications and challenges, and envision the future of this rapidly evolving field. As you read these pages, I encourage you to think boldly and creatively about how real-time analytics can transform not just your work but the world around you. Data is no longer just a resource; it is a catalyst for change. Let us unlock its potential and shape the future of data-driven intelligence, together.

CHAPTER 1
The Foundations of Real-Time Analytics

In a world where data drives decision-making, the ability to act on information as it happens is no longer a luxury; it is a necessity. Real-time analytics has revolutionized the way businesses operate, governments serve their citizens, and individuals interact with technology. It is the process of analyzing data as it is generated, providing insights that can be acted upon almost instantaneously. Unlike traditional analytics, which often involves batch processing and delayed insights, real-time analytics emphasizes speed and immediacy. It allows organizations to monitor, analyze, and respond to data in real time, enabling faster decision-making and improved operational efficiency. This transformative capability forms the foundation for numerous innovations across industries.

Real-time analytics differs from traditional approaches in its immediacy and scale. Historically, data analysis was limited by technology. In the early days of computing, batch processing was the norm, and organizations relied on periodic updates to inform their decisions. While this approach was sufficient in static environments, it became inadequate as the pace of business and technology accelerated. The advent of high-speed internet, cloud computing, and advancements in processing power paved the way for real-time analytics. Today, organizations have access to tools and platforms capable of analyzing vast amounts of data in milliseconds, making insights more actionable than ever before.

One of the defining characteristics of real-time analytics is its ability to provide immediate feedback. Insights are generated as data streams in from various sources, such as sensors, user interactions, or transactional systems. This capability is powered by a continuous flow of data that must be ingested, processed, and visualized in near-instantaneous cycles. The speed and accuracy of these systems are critical, especially in industries where delays could mean lost opportunities or significant risks. For example, financial institutions rely on real-time analytics to detect fraudulent transactions and manage risks, while healthcare providers use it to monitor patient vitals and predict health outcomes.

The applications of real-time analytics are vast and varied, touching nearly every sector of the global economy. In retail, it enables businesses to tailor marketing campaigns and optimize inventory based on current demand. In transportation, it improves traffic management and enhances logistics efficiency. In the energy sector, it facilitates grid operations and predicts equipment failures, ensuring stability and reliability. The ability to deliver personalized experiences is another significant advantage. Companies can use real-time data to understand consumer behavior, offering tailored recommendations and improving customer satisfaction. This level of immediacy and relevance is increasingly critical in today's hyper-competitive market environment.

While the benefits of real-time analytics are undeniable, implementing it comes with challenges. One of the most significant hurdles is ensuring the quality of data. Real-time systems rely on accurate and consistent information; errors or inconsistencies can lead to misleading insights and poor decision-making. Another challenge is the infrastructure required to support these systems. Real-time analytics demands robust processing frameworks, storage solutions, and visualization tools, which can be resource-intensive to build and maintain. Achieving low latency in data processing is also a technical challenge, as even minor delays can undermine the value of real-time insights. Furthermore, security is a critical concern. With data flowing rapidly through pipelines, safeguarding sensitive information against breaches and ensuring compliance with regulations such as GDPR and CCPA becomes paramount.

Despite these challenges, the value of real-time analytics in the digital economy cannot be overstated. It is a cornerstone of innovation, enabling organizations to adapt to rapidly changing conditions and seize opportunities as they arise. In industries where competition is fierce, the ability to act on real-time insights provides a distinct advantage. For governments, it enhances the ability to allocate resources efficiently and respond swiftly to emergencies. Even on an individual level, real-time analytics powers tools and services that simplify everyday life, from traffic updates to fitness tracking apps.

The evolution of real-time analytics represents a shift in how organizations approach decision-making. Rather than relying on retrospective analysis, businesses can now leverage data as it is generated, aligning strategies with the current moment. This shift requires a new mindset, one that prioritizes agility and embraces the complexities of real-time systems. As technology continues to advance, the potential of real-time analytics will only grow, unlocking new opportunities for innovation and impact.

Understanding the foundations of real-time analytics is essential for anyone looking to thrive in today's data-driven world. It is not just about the tools and technologies but also about recognizing the strategic value of immediacy and relevance. Real-time analytics not only transforms the decision-making process but also reshapes the expectations placed on organizations and systems. Businesses today are no longer judged solely on their ability to deliver quality products or services; they are also evaluated on how quickly they can respond to change. This heightened expectation is especially evident in consumer-facing industries, where customers demand instant gratification. Whether it's tracking the delivery of an online purchase, receiving tailored recommendations in a streaming app, or getting live updates on a flight, the expectation for immediacy drives innovation and the adoption of real-time analytics.

At the heart of real-time analytics is a well-designed data pipeline. This pipeline serves as the backbone for collecting, processing, and delivering data insights in real time. The process begins with data ingestion, which involves capturing information from various sources, including sensors, application logs, transactional systems, and social media feeds. Data ingestion must be seamless and continuous to ensure no information is lost. Once ingested, data moves into the processing phase, where it is transformed and analyzed using algorithms, statistical models, or machine learning techniques. This phase often involves leverages distributed computing frameworks such as Apache Kafka, Apache Flink, or Spark Streaming, which are designed to handle large volumes of data with low latency. Finally, insights are delivered to users through visualization tools or automated actions, such as triggering alerts or executing system updates.

The success of real-time analytics hinges on several critical factors. First is the speed of processing, often referred to as latency. Low latency is essential to delivering insights quickly enough to be actionable. For example, in financial markets, delays of even milliseconds can result in missed opportunities or significant losses. Second is the scalability of the system. As organizations grow and their data sources expand, real-time systems must be capable of handling increasing volumes and complexity without degradation in performance. Third is the reliability of the system. Real-time analytics cannot afford frequent downtimes or inaccuracies, as these could undermine trust and render the insights unusable.

Real-time analytics also brings profound implications for how organizations approach strategy and operations. Traditionally, decisions were based on historical data, with strategies crafted to address past trends. While this approach provided a solid foundation, it often lacked the agility to address emerging challenges or capitalize on new opportunities. Real-time analytics shifts this paradigm by enabling organizations to adopt a more proactive and dynamic approach. For instance, a retail company using real-time analytics can monitor sales trends and customer behavior to adjust pricing or inventory levels on the fly, ensuring they stay ahead of competitors. Similarly, a logistics company can use live data to optimize delivery routes, saving time and resources while improving customer satisfaction.

The role of real-time analytics extends beyond operational efficiency; it also enhances the customer experience in meaningful ways. Modern consumers expect interactions with businesses to be seamless, personalized, and immediate. Real-time analytics enables companies to meet these expectations by analyzing user behavior and preferences at the moment. For example, a streaming service can recommend content based on a user's viewing habits as they navigate the platform, while an e-commerce site can suggest complementary products based on items in a shopper's cart. These tailored experiences not only increase engagement but also foster loyalty, giving businesses a competitive edge.

Despite its many advantages, real-time analytics is not without its challenges. One of the most pressing concerns is the ethical use of data. As organizations collect and analyze data in real time, they must ensure they respect user privacy and comply with legal regulations. Misuse of data can lead to public backlash, legal penalties, and a loss of trust, which can be difficult to recover from. Another challenge is the high cost associated with building and maintaining real-time systems. The infrastructure required for real-time analytics such as distributed computing frameworks, high-speed storage solutions, and advanced processing tools can be expensive, particularly for small and medium-sized businesses. However, advancements in cloud computing have begun to lower these barriers, making real-time analytics more accessible to a broader range of organizations.

The growing adoption of real-time analytics is also driving innovation in technology and methodology. Artificial intelligence and machine learning are increasingly being integrated into real-time systems, enhancing their ability to provide predictive insights and automated decision-making. Edge computing, which processes data closer to its source rather than in a centralized location, is another emerging trend that reduces latency and improves the efficiency of real-time systems. These advancements are shaping the future of real-time analytics, ensuring it remains a critical tool for organizations navigating a fast-paced and data-rich world.

1.1 Understanding the Real-Time Analytics Ecosystem

While we have discussed the foundations of real-time analytics, it is essential to take a closer look at the ecosystem that powers these systems. Real-time analytics does not exist in isolation—it is a complex interplay of technologies, workflows, and human expertise. At the core of this ecosystem are the data sources, which can range from sensors in IoT devices to transaction logs from e-commerce platforms. The diversity of these data sources highlights the flexibility and adaptability required of real-time systems. They must be capable of ingesting structured, semi-structured, and unstructured data at scale, often from multiple sources simultaneously.

The role of processing frameworks in the ecosystem is equally critical. These frameworks act as the engine of real-time analytics, handling the heavy lifting of transforming raw data into actionable insights. Tools such as Apache Kafka, Apache Flink, and Spark Streaming are widely used because of their ability to handle massive data streams with low latency. However, the choice of a processing framework depends on the specific needs of the organization, such as the volume of data, the complexity of transformations, and the desired speed of output. In addition to processing frameworks, real-time analytics systems rely on robust storage solutions to manage the influx of data. Storage technologies like NoSQL databases and in-memory data grids are popular for their ability to support fast read-and-write operations.

Visualization tools complete the ecosystem by presenting insights in a manner that is both accessible and actionable. Dashboards, alerts, and reports are tailored to meet the needs of different stakeholders, from executives requiring high-level summaries to analysts seeking detailed trends. The ecosystem's success relies on seamless integration among its components. Organizations must ensure that their systems are not only technologically sound but also aligned with their strategic goals. A misalignment between technology and business objectives can lead to underutilized systems and wasted investments.

1.2 Human Expertise and Its Role in Real-Time Analytics

While technology forms the backbone of real-time analytics, human expertise is the glue that holds it all together. No matter how advanced a system may be, its true value depends on the people who design, operate, and interpret it. Data scientists, engineers, and analysts play a pivotal role in creating workflows, optimizing algorithms, and ensuring the accuracy of insights. These professionals are responsible for bridging the gap between raw data and actionable decisions, often working collaboratively to address challenges and identify opportunities.

One of the critical skills required in real-time analytics is the ability to interpret data within context. Insights generated by a system are only as useful as the understanding and decisions they inspire. For example, an e-commerce business receiving a real-time alert about a surge in product demand must decide how to respond—whether to adjust pricing, allocate inventory, or launch a marketing campaign. This decision-making process requires domain knowledge, critical thinking, and an understanding of broader market dynamics.

Another aspect of human expertise lies in system design and optimization. Building a real-time analytics system involves making trade-offs between speed, accuracy, and cost. For instance, achieving ultra-low latency may require higher investments in infrastructure, while maximizing accuracy could slow down processing times. Experts must balance these competing priorities to create systems that meet organizational needs without overextending resources.

Training and upskilling are essential to maintaining the human element in real-time analytics. As technologies evolve, professionals must stay updated on emerging tools, methodologies, and best practices. Organizations that invest in their teams' development are more likely to reap the full benefits of real-time analytics. Furthermore, fostering a culture of curiosity and innovation encourages employees to explore creative solutions and maximize the potential of data-driven insights.

Finally, ethical considerations are a significant part of the human role in real-time analytics. Professionals must navigate complex issues related to data privacy, security, and fairness. Decisions about what data to collect, how to use it, and how to protect it have far-reaching implications for organizations and society. Ensuring that real-time analytics systems operate within ethical and legal boundaries is a responsibility that requires both technical and moral judgment.

By diving deeper into the ecosystem of real-time analytics and the indispensable role of human expertise, we gain a more comprehensive understanding of what it takes to build and sustain these systems. Technology provides the tools, but it is the strategic alignment, skilled professionals, and ethical frameworks that ensure real-time analytics delivers on their promise. These elements are just as important as the insights themselves, forming a foundation for future exploration in the chapters to come.

OLUSHOLA IBRAHIM

CHAPTER 2
Understanding Real-Time Data Pipelines

Real-time data pipelines are the lifeblood of real-time analytics systems. They are responsible for the seamless flow of data from its point of origin to its final destination, where it is transformed into actionable insights. Understanding the architecture and functionality of these pipelines is crucial for organizations looking to harness the power of real-time analytics. This chapter delves into the components of real-time data pipelines, their design principles, and the tools that enable them to operate efficiently and reliably.

At the core of a real-time data pipeline is its ability to ingest, process, and deliver data at high speed. The process begins with data ingestion, which involves collecting information from a variety of sources. These sources can include IoT sensors, social media platforms, transactional systems, and application logs, among others. The challenge of data ingestion lies in its diversity and volume. Different sources may produce data in varying formats and at different rates, requiring the pipeline to be highly flexible and scalable. Tools like Apache Kafka, a distributed event-streaming platform, are widely used for their ability to handle large-scale data ingestion with low latency.

Once data is ingested, it moves into the processing stage, where it is transformed into a format that can be analyzed and acted upon. This stage often involves cleaning, enriching, and aggregating data to ensure its quality and relevance. For example, raw sensor data may be cleaned to remove outliers, enriched with contextual information such as timestamps or geolocation, and aggregated to produce meaningful metrics. Processing frameworks like Apache Flink and Spark Streaming play a critical role in this stage, enabling organizations to handle complex transformations in real time. These frameworks are designed to operate on distributed systems, allowing them to process large volumes of data efficiently.

The final stage of a real-time data pipeline is data delivery, where processed insights are sent to their intended destinations. This could involve updating a dashboard, triggering an alert, or feeding data into a machine learning model for further analysis. Delivery mechanisms must ensure that insights reach the right stakeholders in a timely and secure manner. Visualization tools like Tableau or Power BI are often used to present insights in a user-friendly format, while APIs and messaging systems facilitate integration with other applications.

Designing an effective real-time data pipeline requires careful consideration of several principles. One of the most important is fault tolerance, which ensures that the pipeline can recover from failures without losing data or compromising performance. Distributed systems are inherently prone to issues such as hardware failures, network interruptions, and software bugs, making fault tolerance a critical feature. Another key principle is scalability. As organizations grow and their data sources expand, the pipeline must be capable of handling increased volumes and complexity without degradation in performance. This often involves designing pipelines with modular components that can be scaled independently as needed.

Latency is another crucial consideration in pipeline design. Low latency is essential for ensuring that insights are delivered quickly enough to be actionable. Achieving this requires optimizing every stage of the pipeline, from data ingestion to processing and delivery. For example, using in-memory processing can significantly reduce the time required for data transformations, while leveraging caching mechanisms can speed up data retrieval. However, reducing latency often involves trade-offs with other factors, such as cost and system complexity. Organizations must balance these trade-offs based on their specific needs and priorities.

Security is a fundamental aspect of real-time data pipelines, particularly as data flows through multiple systems and environments. Pipelines must be designed to protect sensitive information from unauthorized access, breaches, and misuse. This includes implementing encryption for data in transit and at rest, as well as access controls to ensure that only authorized personnel can interact with the pipeline. Compliance with regulations such as GDPR and CCPA is also essential, particularly for organizations handling personal or financial data.

The choice of tools and technologies for building real-time data pipelines plays a significant role in their success. In addition to the previously mentioned Apache Kafka, Flink, and Spark Streaming, other popular tools include RabbitMQ, a messaging broker for managing communication between systems, and Redis, an in-memory data structure store that supports real-time analytics. The selection of tools depends on factors such as the volume of data, the complexity of processing requirements, and the organization's existing technology stack.

Real-time data pipelines are not just technical systems; they are strategic assets that enable organizations to operate more efficiently and effectively. They provide the infrastructure for applications ranging from fraud detection and predictive maintenance to personalized marketing and real-time decision-making. As such, designing and managing these pipelines requires a combination of technical expertise, strategic vision, and a commitment to continuous improvement.

Real-time data pipelines are the foundation upon which real-time analytics systems are built. They enable the seamless flow of data from its source to its destination, transforming raw information into actionable insights. By understanding the components, design principles, and tools that make up these pipelines, organizations can unlock the full potential of real-time analytics and position themselves for success in a data-driven world. Real-time data pipelines are not just about processing and delivering data quickly; they are also a living ecosystem that evolves with the needs of the business and the advancements in technology. Organizations that understand this dynamic nature can leverage their pipelines to create competitive advantages. For instance, the integration of machine learning into data pipelines is becoming increasingly common. By embedding predictive models directly into the pipeline, organizations can go beyond descriptive analytics to predict future outcomes and automate decision-making processes. For example, in retail, pipelines equipped with machine learning can dynamically adjust prices based on supply, demand, and competitor activity all in real time.

Another transformative trend is the rise of edge computing, which allows data processing to occur closer to its source rather than being sent to a centralized data center. This approach reduces latency significantly, making it ideal for use cases like autonomous vehicles, where every millisecond counts, or in industrial IoT systems, where equipment, health and efficiency need constant monitoring. By processing data at the edge, real-time pipelines can deliver insights faster while reducing the load on central servers and networks.

Data governance is another aspect that often gets overlooked but plays a vital role in real-time pipelines. As data flows rapidly through various systems, ensuring its integrity, quality, and compliance becomes a critical challenge. Data governance frameworks must be integrated into pipelines to track data lineage, maintain accuracy, and comply with regulations. This involves automating processes such as data validation, deduplication, and enrichment within the pipeline to ensure that the insights generated are reliable and actionable. For organizations operating in regulated industries, such as finance or healthcare, robust data governance is non-negotiable and forms a key component of the pipeline design.

The orchestration of real-time data pipelines is another area that demands attention. Orchestration tools, such as Apache Airflow and Prefect, help manage the dependencies and workflows within the pipeline, ensuring that data flows smoothly from one stage to the next. These tools are particularly valuable in complex systems where data from multiple sources needs to be processed and delivered to various destinations simultaneously. Effective orchestration not only improves the efficiency of the pipeline but also makes it easier to monitor and troubleshoot issues, reducing downtime and improving reliability.

Collaboration between teams is essential for the successful implementation and operation of real-time data pipelines. Building and maintaining these pipelines requires input from data engineers, data scientists, business analysts, and IT operations. Each team brings unique expertise to the table, from designing the architecture and writing the code to interpreting the data and aligning it with business objectives. Open communication and shared goals are crucial for ensuring that the pipeline meets both technical and strategic requirements. Agile methodologies, which emphasize collaboration, adaptability, and iterative improvement, are particularly well-suited to the development of real-time systems.

As organizations scale their operations, the complexity of real-time pipelines can grow exponentially. Managing this complexity requires not just technological solutions but also a cultural shift within the organization. Leaders must prioritize data literacy, ensuring that employees at all levels understand the value of data and how to use it effectively. Training programs, workshops, and cross-functional teams can help foster a culture where data-driven decision-making is the norm.

Real-time pipelines also open up new possibilities for innovation. By providing instant access to insights, they enable organizations to experiment with new business models, optimize existing processes, and create personalized customer experiences. For example, a media streaming platform might use real-time data to analyze viewer preferences and deliver targeted recommendations, while a logistics company could use it to monitor fleet performance and optimize delivery routes. These innovations are not just about improving efficiency but also about creating new value for customers and stakeholders.

Despite their transformative potential, real-time pipelines are not without their limitations. One of the biggest challenges is the cost associated with building and maintaining these systems. High-performance infrastructure, skilled personnel, and ongoing updates can place a significant financial burden on organizations, particularly small and medium-sized businesses. However, the emergence of cloud computing and managed services is helping to reduce these barriers. Platforms like AWS Kinesis, Google Cloud Dataflow, and Azure Stream Analytics offer scalable, pay-as-you-go solutions that make real-time analytics more accessible. These services also handle much of the complexity behind the scenes, allowing organizations to focus on deriving value from their data rather than managing infrastructure.

Another limitation is the inherent trade-offs in system design. For example, optimizing for low latency might compromise accuracy, while prioritizing fault tolerance could increase costs. Organizations must carefully evaluate these trade-offs to align their pipelines with their specific goals and constraints. This requires a deep understanding of both the technical aspects of pipeline design and the strategic priorities of the business.

2.1 The Role of Real-Time Pipelines in Data Democratization

Real-time data pipelines are not just tools for delivering insights quickly; they are also powerful enablers of data democratization within organizations. Traditionally, access to data and analytics has been confined to specific departments, such as IT or data science teams. However, real-time pipelines are breaking down these silos by providing actionable insights to a wider range of stakeholders in real-time. With user-friendly dashboards, real-time alerts, and embedded analytics, decision-makers across various functions—such as marketing, operations, and customer support—can access the data they need without relying on technical teams.

This democratization is further fueled by self-service analytics platforms that integrate seamlessly with real-time pipelines. These platforms allow non-technical users to explore data, generate reports, and uncover trends without writing a single line of code. For example, a sales team can use real-time insights to track their performance metrics during a campaign, while customer support teams can monitor sentiment data to adjust their responses. By empowering employees with the right tools and data, organizations can foster a culture of agility and informed decision-making at every level.

Data democratization through real-time pipelines also reduces bottlenecks in workflows, enabling faster responses to opportunities and challenges. For instance, in the retail industry, store managers can adjust pricing or promotions on the fly based on real-time sales data, rather than waiting for end-of-day reports. Similarly, in logistics, warehouse managers can reallocate resources to high-demand areas as soon as bottlenecks are detected. This level of agility is critical in a fast-paced world where delays can lead to lost revenue or customer dissatisfaction.

However, democratizing real-time data comes with its own challenges. One of the most significant is ensuring data literacy across the organization. While providing access to data is essential, employees must also understand how to interpret and act on the insights they receive. This requires ongoing training and support, as well as a clear governance framework to ensure data is used responsibly and ethically. Organizations must strike a balance between empowering employees with data and maintaining control over sensitive information.

2.2 Environmental and Ethical Implications of Real-Time Data Pipelines

While the focus of real-time data pipelines is often on their technical and business benefits, it is equally important to consider their environmental and ethical implications. Real-time systems require significant computational resources to process large volumes of data at high speed. This demand can lead to increased energy consumption, particularly when pipelines rely on data centers and cloud infrastructure. As organizations scale their real-time analytics capabilities, the environmental footprint of these systems becomes a growing concern.

To address this, organizations can adopt sustainable practices, such as optimizing their pipelines for energy efficiency or using cloud providers that prioritize renewable energy. For example, implementing batch processing for non-critical tasks alongside real-time pipelines can reduce computational load and energy consumption. Similarly, leveraging serverless architectures can help organizations scale their resources dynamically, ensuring they only use what is needed at any given time. By adopting these practices, businesses can minimize their environmental impact while still reaping the benefits of real-time analytics.

Ethical considerations are another critical aspect of real-time pipelines. As organizations collect and analyze data in real time, they must ensure that they do so in a way that respects user privacy and complies with regulations. The speed and volume of data in real-time pipelines can make it challenging to implement safeguards, but this is no excuse for negligence. Companies must invest in robust encryption, anonymization techniques, and access controls to protect sensitive information. Furthermore, transparency is key organizations that must clearly communicate how they collect, use, and store data to build trust with their stakeholders.

Bias in real-time analytics is another ethical concern that requires attention. Algorithms used in pipelines can unintentionally perpetuate biases present in the data, leading to unfair outcomes or discriminatory practices. For instance, in hiring platforms, real-time recommendations based on biased historical data could disadvantage certain groups. To mitigate this, organizations must rigorously test their algorithms for fairness and ensure that diverse perspectives are included in the development process. Regular audits and external reviews can also help identify and address biases in real-time systems.

Real-time pipelines are also at the forefront of ethical dilemmas in surveillance and monitoring. While these systems are invaluable for detecting fraud, enhancing security, or optimizing operations, their misuse can lead to intrusive monitoring or violations of individual rights. For example, in workplace analytics, real-time systems that track employee productivity must balance performance measurement with respect for privacy. Organizations must develop clear policies and guidelines to ensure their use of real-time pipelines aligns with ethical principles and societal expectations.

By addressing the broader implications of real-time pipelines, including data democratization, environmental impact, and ethical considerations, we gain a more holistic view of their role in modern organizations. These systems are not just technical achievements; they are transformative tools with far-reaching consequences for business, society, and the environment. As organizations continue to innovate in this space, they must do so responsibly, ensuring that the benefits of real-time analytics are balanced with their broader obligations.

OLUSHOLA IBRAHIM

CHAPTER 3
The Role of Cloud Computing in Real-Time Analytics

The advent of cloud computing has transformed the way organizations approach real-time analytics. By providing scalable, flexible, and cost-efficient infrastructure, the cloud has made it possible to process vast amounts of data in real time, enabling businesses to extract actionable insights faster than ever before. This chapter explores how cloud computing amplifies the capabilities of real-time analytics, the leading cloud platforms that dominate the space, and the opportunities and challenges associated with adopting cloud-based solutions.

Cloud computing serves as the backbone for many real-time analytics systems. Unlike traditional on-premises infrastructure, which requires significant upfront investment and ongoing maintenance, cloud platforms offer a pay-as-you-go model that reduces capital expenditure. This financial flexibility is particularly beneficial for small and medium-sized enterprises (SMEs) that may lack the resources to build and maintain their own data centers. Additionally, the cloud's scalability ensures that organizations can handle sudden spikes in data volume without compromising performance. For instance, an e-commerce platform can scale its cloud resources dynamically during a flash sale, ensuring real-time analytics continues to operate seamlessly.

One of the most significant contributions of cloud computing to real-time analytics is its ability to unify diverse data sources. In today's interconnected world, businesses generate data from numerous touchpoints, including customer interactions, IoT devices, social media platforms, and supply chain systems. Cloud platforms act as a central hub, aggregating data from these sources and making it available for real-time processing. This integration capability is critical for organizations aiming to achieve a 360-degree view of their operations and customers. Tools like AWS Glue, Google Cloud Dataflow, and Azure Data Factory are designed specifically to streamline data integration and pipeline orchestration in the cloud.

Cloud platforms also provide a wide array of services and tools that are purpose-built for real-time analytics. For example, AWS Kinesis, Azure Stream Analytics, and Google Cloud Pub/Sub enable organizations to ingest and process data streams in real time. These services come with built-in capabilities such as auto-scaling, fault tolerance, and real-time monitoring, which significantly reduce the complexity of managing real-time pipelines. Moreover, cloud providers often offer machine learning and artificial intelligence services that can be seamlessly integrated into analytics workflows. These tools empower organizations to perform predictive and prescriptive analytics in real time, opening up new possibilities for innovation and efficiency.

Security and compliance are critical considerations when adopting cloud-based real-time analytics. While cloud providers invest heavily in securing their infrastructure, the responsibility for securing data within the cloud often falls on the organization. This shared responsibility model requires businesses to implement robust access controls, encryption, and monitoring solutions to protect sensitive information. Additionally, organizations must ensure compliance with regulations such as GDPR, HIPAA, and CCPA, particularly if they operate in regulated industries like finance or healthcare. Cloud providers often offer compliance certifications and tools to help businesses meet these requirements, but organizations must remain vigilant in managing their data governance policies.

Another advantage of cloud computing is its role in enabling real-time analytics on a global scale. With data centers distributed across multiple regions, cloud platforms allow organizations to process and analyze data close to its source, reducing latency and improving performance. This capability is particularly valuable for businesses with a global presence, such as streaming platforms or logistics companies, which need to deliver real-time insights to users across different geographies. By leveraging the cloud's global reach, organizations can ensure consistent and reliable performance, even in the face of complex data distribution challenges.

The cloud has also democratized access to real-time analytics by lowering the barriers to entry. Previously, only large enterprises with significant financial and technical resources could afford the infrastructure required for real-time analytics. Today, cloud platforms offer affordable and easy-to-use services that make these capabilities accessible to businesses of all sizes. This democratization has spurred innovation across industries, with startups and SMEs using real-time analytics to disrupt traditional business models and compete with larger players. For example, a small logistics company might use cloud-based analytics to optimize delivery routes and reduce fuel costs, leveling the playing field with industry giants.

However, the adoption of cloud-based real-time analytics is not without its challenges. One of the most significant is the potential for vendor lock-in, where organizations become heavily dependent on a single cloud provider's ecosystem. This reliance can limit flexibility and make it difficult to switch providers or adopt hybrid solutions. To mitigate this risk, many organizations are adopting multi-cloud strategies, using services from multiple providers to diversify their capabilities and reduce dependency. While this approach adds complexity, it also provides greater flexibility and resilience.

Cost management is another challenge in cloud-based real-time analytics. While the pay-as-you-go model offers financial flexibility, it can also lead to unexpected expenses if resources are not managed carefully. Organizations must implement cost-monitoring tools and best practices to avoid overruns and ensure they are maximizing the value of their cloud investments. Additionally, understanding the pricing models of different cloud services is essential for making informed decisions about which tools and solutions to adopt.

Despite these challenges, the benefits of cloud computing for real-time analytics far outweigh the drawbacks. The cloud's scalability, flexibility, and rich ecosystem of tools have made it an indispensable enabler of real-time insights. Organizations that embrace cloud-based real-time analytics are better positioned to respond to market changes, optimize their operations, and deliver exceptional customer experiences.

Cloud computing has revolutionized real-time analytics by providing the infrastructure, tools, and scalability needed to handle the demands of modern data-driven businesses. By leveraging the cloud, organizations can overcome the limitations of traditional infrastructure and unlock new opportunities for growth and innovation. The impact of cloud computing on real-time analytics extends beyond just scalability and cost-efficiency; it also reshapes how organizations approach innovation and collaboration. In the past, implementing real-time analytics required significant lead time, as teams needed to acquire hardware, configure software, and ensure compatibility with existing systems. The cloud eliminates much of this complexity by offering ready-to-use services that can be deployed within minutes. This acceleration of deployment cycles allows organizations to experiment with new ideas, iterate rapidly, and bring innovations to market faster. For example, a retail company might test new pricing algorithms in real time during a seasonal sale, using cloud-based analytics to measure their impact on revenue and customer behavior.

The flexibility of cloud computing also fosters collaboration across departments and geographies. By centralizing data and analytics capabilities in the cloud, organizations can break down silos and enable cross-functional teams to work together seamlessly. For instance, marketing teams can collaborate with data scientists to analyze campaign performance in real time, while product managers and engineers can use live feedback to optimize features and functionality. This level of collaboration not only improves operational efficiency but also drives creativity and innovation by enabling diverse perspectives to contribute to problem-solving.

Another critical advantage of cloud computing is its ability to support disaster recovery and business continuity in real-time analytics. Data pipelines and analytics systems are vulnerable to disruptions caused by hardware failures, cyberattacks, or natural disasters. Cloud platforms mitigate these risks by offering built-in redundancy and failover mechanisms. For example, data replication across multiple regions ensures that insights remain accessible even if one data center goes offline.

Similarly, automated backups and recovery tools enable organizations to quickly restore their systems in the event of an outage. This resilience is particularly important for industries that rely heavily on real-time analytics, such as finance, healthcare, and logistics, where downtime can have significant consequences.

Cloud computing is also driving the adoption of edge computing, a paradigm that complements real-time analytics by processing data closer to its source. Edge computing reduces the need to transmit large volumes of data to centralized cloud servers, thereby minimizing latency and bandwidth usage. This approach is particularly beneficial for applications that require ultra-fast decision-making, such as autonomous vehicles, industrial automation, and smart cities. By integrating edge and cloud capabilities, organizations can create hybrid systems that combine the speed of local processing with the scalability of centralized analytics. For example, an energy company might use edge devices to monitor equipment performance in real time and send aggregated insights to the cloud for long-term analysis and strategic planning.

However, the widespread adoption of cloud-based real-time analytics also raises questions about data sovereignty and regulatory compliance. Many countries have laws requiring certain types of data to remain within their borders, which can complicate the use of global cloud platforms. Organizations must navigate these regulations carefully, often working with cloud providers to ensure compliance. For instance, some cloud platforms offer region-specific services that allow organizations to store and process data within designated jurisdictions. These localized solutions help businesses comply with regulations while still benefiting from the advantages of the cloud.

Additionally, cloud computing is driving advancements in artificial intelligence (AI) and machine learning (ML) for real-time analytics. Cloud platforms provide pre-trained models, AI-powered tools, and computing resources that make it easier for organizations to integrate machine learning into their analytics workflows. For example, a financial institution might use a cloud-based ML model to detect fraudulent transactions in real time, flagging suspicious activity for further investigation. Similarly, a healthcare provider could deploy AI-powered diagnostics to analyze patient data and identify potential health risks as they emerge. These capabilities are democratizing access to advanced analytics, enabling businesses of all sizes to leverage innovative technology.

The environmental implications of cloud computing are another aspect worth exploring. While the cloud offers significant efficiencies compared to traditional on-premises infrastructure, its energy consumption remains a concern. Data centers that power cloud platforms require substantial electricity, much of which is still generated from non-renewable sources. To address this, leading cloud providers are investing in renewable energy projects and implementing energy-efficient technologies. For example, some providers use advanced cooling systems to reduce the energy required to keep data centers operational. By prioritizing sustainability, organizations can align their real-time analytics initiatives with broader environmental goals, contributing to a greener future.

3.1 Enhancing Real-Time Analytics Through Hybrid Cloud Solutions

While public cloud platforms have revolutionized real-time analytics, hybrid cloud solutions are emerging as a powerful alternative for organizations with unique needs. A hybrid cloud combines the scalability and flexibility of public clouds with the control and customization of private clouds or on-premises infrastructure. This approach is particularly beneficial for industries with strict regulatory requirements, sensitive data, or legacy systems that cannot be fully migrated to the public cloud.

For example, a financial institution might store highly sensitive customer data in its private cloud while leveraging a public cloud for real-time analytics on anonymized datasets. This setup ensures compliance with data protection laws while still benefiting from the scalability and advanced analytics capabilities of the public cloud. Similarly, manufacturing companies using Internet of Things (IoT) devices can process critical data at the edge or in private clouds close to their facilities, while using public clouds for broader trend analysis and predictive maintenance.

Hybrid cloud solutions also offer cost optimization opportunities. Organizations can strategically allocate workloads between private and public clouds based on cost, performance, and security considerations. For instance, seasonal spikes in data volume such as during holiday sales or major events can be handled by the public cloud, while routine operations are managed in-house to reduce expenses. This dynamic allocation of resources ensures that businesses maintain optimal performance without overpaying for unused capacity.

However, adopting a hybrid cloud model requires careful planning and robust orchestration. Data synchronization between private and public clouds can be challenging, especially in real-time analytics where latency is critical. Organizations must implement tools and frameworks that facilitate seamless data flow across environments. Cloud providers often offer hybrid solutions such as AWS Outposts, Azure Arc, and Google Anthos, which enable organizations to extend public cloud services to their private environments. These tools simplify integration and help maintain a unified analytics strategy across multiple infrastructures.

3.2 The Role of Cloud-Native Analytics in Real-Time Systems

As real-time analytics evolves, cloud-native technologies are becoming the new standard for designing and deploying analytics systems. Cloud-native refers to applications and services specifically built to leverage the capabilities of cloud platforms, such as microservices architecture, containerization, and serverless computing. These technologies are reshaping how real-time data pipelines are designed, deployed, and scaled, offering unparalleled agility and efficiency.

Microservices architecture plays a significant role in cloud-native analytics. By breaking down monolithic applications into smaller, independently deployable services, organizations can build flexible pipelines that are easier to manage and scale. For example, a real-time analytics pipeline might have separate microservices for data ingestion, transformation, and visualization. Each microservice can be developed, deployed, and updated independently, reducing downtime and enabling faster iterations. This modular approach also allows organizations to experiment with new technologies or integrate third-party services without overhauling their entire system.

Containerization further enhances the efficiency of cloud-native analytics. Tools like Docker and Kubernetes allow organizations to package microservices into lightweight, portable containers that can run consistently across different environments. This portability simplifies the deployment of real-time analytics systems, enabling organizations to move workloads between cloud providers or scale services dynamically based on demand. For instance, during a product launch, containers hosting data processing microservices can be scaled up to handle increased traffic and scaled back down afterward to optimize costs.

Serverless computing takes cloud-native analytics a step further by abstracting the underlying infrastructure entirely. With serverless platforms like AWS Lambda, Azure Functions, or Google Cloud Functions, organizations can focus on writing code for real-time analytics tasks without worrying about managing servers or scaling infrastructure. Serverless computing is particularly well-suited for event-driven analytics, where specific triggers such as a user action or a system alert initiate processing workflows. This approach minimizes idle resource usage and reduces costs, making real-time analytics more accessible to organizations with limited budgets.

Another benefit of cloud-native analytics is its ability to support advanced machine learning workflows. Cloud-native platforms provide seamless integration with AI and ML services, enabling organizations to incorporate predictive and prescriptive analytics into their real-time systems. For example, a logistics company could use cloud-native tools to deploy a machine learning model that predicts delivery delays based on real-time traffic and weather data. By automating these predictions, the company can reroute deliveries proactively, improving efficiency and customer satisfaction.

Despite its advantages, adopting cloud-native technologies requires a shift in mindset and skills. Traditional IT teams must embrace modern DevOps practices, which emphasize collaboration, automation, and continuous delivery. Organizations must also invest in training and upskilling their workforce to navigate the complexities of microservices, containerization, and serverless architectures. By fostering a culture of innovation and learning, businesses can fully capitalize on the potential of cloud-native analytics.

3.3 Cloud Computing as a Catalyst for the Future of Real-Time Analytics

Cloud computing is not just a tool for enhancing real-time analytics—it is a catalyst for its future evolution. As cloud platforms continue to innovate, they are pushing the boundaries of what is possible in real-time data processing. Technologies like quantum computing, 5G connectivity, and federated learning are already being integrated into cloud ecosystems, opening up new possibilities for real-time analytics across industries.

Quantum computing, for instance, holds the potential to revolutionize analytics by solving complex optimization problems and processing massive datasets at unprecedented speeds. Although still in its early stages, cloud providers like IBM and Google are offering quantum computing as a service, allowing organizations to experiment with innovative algorithms. In real-time analytics, quantum computing could enable breakthroughs in areas such as supply chain optimization, financial modeling, and drug discovery.

The rollout of 5G connectivity is another significant change for cloud-based real-time analytics. With its ultra-low latency and high bandwidth, 5G allows data to be collected and processed in real time from a vast array of devices and sensors. This capability is particularly valuable for industries like autonomous vehicles, where split-second decisions are critical, or smart cities, where real-time data from thousands of sensors can improve urban planning and resource allocation.

Federated learning is yet another emerging technology that aligns with cloud computing and real-time analytics. By enabling machine learning models to be trained on decentralized data sources without transferring the data itself, federated learning enhances privacy and reduces the bandwidth required for real-time systems. This approach is ideal for applications like healthcare analytics, where patient data must remain confidential, or mobile applications, where data is distributed across millions of devices.

In conclusion, cloud computing has not only transformed the present state of real-time analytics but is also laying the foundation for its future. By embracing hybrid cloud solutions, cloud-native technologies, and emerging innovations, organizations can stay ahead of the curve and unlock new possibilities for growth and efficiency.

OLUSHOLA IBRAHIM

CHAPTER 4
Real-Time Analytics Use Cases Across Industries

Real-time analytics is no longer a niche technology confined to a handful of industries; it is a transformative tool that touches nearly every sector of the global economy. From retail to healthcare, finance to logistics, real-time analytics is enabling organizations to optimize operations, enhance customer experiences, and uncover new revenue streams. This chapter explores practical applications of real-time analytics across diverse industries, showcasing how organizations leverage their capabilities to solve problems and create value.

In the retail industry, real-time analytics has become a cornerstone for enhancing customer experiences and driving sales. With the rise of e-commerce and omnichannel retailing, businesses must adapt to rapidly changing consumer preferences and behaviors. Real-time analytics enables retailers to track customer interactions across multiple channels, providing insights that inform personalized recommendations, targeted promotions, and dynamic pricing strategies. For example, an online retailer might use real-time data to identify trends in product demand during a flash sale, adjusting prices and inventory allocation to maximize revenue. Brick-and-mortar stores are also benefiting from real-time analytics by using sensors and video analytics to monitor foot traffic and optimize store layouts.

In healthcare, real-time analytics is saving lives by enabling faster and more accurate decision-making. Hospitals and clinics use real-time data from patient monitoring devices to detect early signs of deterioration, allowing medical teams to intervene promptly. For instance, wearable devices that track heart rate, blood pressure, and oxygen levels can send alerts to healthcare providers if a patient's vital signs deviate from normal ranges.

Real-time analytics is also transforming public health by enabling governments and organizations to track the spread of diseases and allocate resources more effectively. During the COVID-19 pandemic, real-time analytics played a crucial role in monitoring infection rates, predicting hospital capacity needs, and guiding vaccination efforts.

The finance industry has long been a leader in adopting real-time analytics, particularly in areas like fraud detection and risk management. Financial institutions process millions of transactions daily, making it critical to identify suspicious activity as it occurs. Real-time analytics enables banks to flag anomalies, such as unusual spending patterns or multiple failed logins attempts and take immediate action to prevent fraud. Additionally, real-time analytics powers algorithmic trading, where investment decisions are made in fractions of a second based on live market data. This capability has revolutionized the way financial markets operate, giving traders an edge in a highly competitive environment.

Logistics and supply chain management are other domains where real-time analytics is driving significant improvements. Companies in this sector face complex challenges, such as fluctuating demand, unpredictable delays, and the need for efficient resource allocation. Real-time analytics provides visibility into every stage of the supply chain, from inventory levels to delivery times, enabling organizations to respond swiftly to disruptions. For example, a logistics company might use real-time GPS data to reroute deliveries around traffic congestion, ensuring timely arrivals and reducing fuel costs. Similarly, manufacturers can use real-time analytics to monitor equipment performance and schedule maintenance proactively, minimizing downtime and maximizing productivity.

The energy sector is also harnessing the power of real-time analytics to optimize operations and support sustainability initiatives. Utility companies use real-time data from smart meters to monitor energy consumption patterns and balance supply with demand. This capability is particularly valuable during peak usage periods, helping to prevent blackouts and reduce energy waste. Real-time analytics also plays a key role in renewable energy management, where it is used to predict and respond to fluctuations in energy generation from solar and wind sources. For instance, a wind farm might use real-time weather data to adjust turbine settings for optimal performance, while a solar energy provider could use live data to manage energy storage and distribution.

In the transportation industry, real-time analytics is revolutionizing everything from public transit systems to ride-sharing platforms. Cities are using real-time data to improve traffic flow, reduce congestion, and enhance public safety. For example, traffic management systems powered by real-time analytics can adjust signal timings based on live traffic conditions, reducing delays and emissions. Ride-sharing companies like Uber and Lyft rely on real-time data to match drivers with passengers, optimize routes, and predict demand in different areas. These capabilities not only improve operational efficiency but also enhance the user experience by reducing waiting times and ensuring reliable service.

The entertainment and media industry has also embraced real-time analytics to engage audiences and drive revenue. Streaming platforms like Netflix and Spotify use real-time data to deliver personalized content recommendations, keeping users engaged and satisfied. Live sports broadcasters leverage real-time analytics to provide viewers with instant insights, such as player statistics, game predictions, and heatmaps, enhancing the overall viewing experience. Additionally, real-time analytics is being used in advertising to deliver targeted ads to viewers based on their preferences and behavior, increasing the effectiveness of campaigns.

Even the public sector is finding innovative ways to apply real-time analytics. Governments are using real-time data to improve public services, enhance disaster response, and increase transparency. For instance, smart city initiatives often rely on real-time analytics to manage traffic, monitor air quality, and optimize waste collection. During emergencies, such as natural disasters, real-time analytics helps first responders coordinate rescue efforts and allocate resources where they are needed most. By leveraging real-time insights, governments can make more informed decisions and deliver better outcomes for their citizens.

The gaming industry is another area where real-time analytics is having a profound impact. Game developers use real-time data to monitor player behavior, optimize game mechanics, and deliver personalized experiences. For example, a multiplayer online game might use real-time analytics to match players with opponents of similar skill levels, ensuring a fair and enjoyable experience. Additionally, game publishers can use live data to identify and address technical issues, such as server lags or crashes, improving overall performance and user satisfaction.

Real-time analytics is also making strides in education, where it is being used to enhance learning outcomes and improve institutional efficiency. Educational platforms can use real-time data to track student progress, identify areas of difficulty, and provide personalized feedback. For instance, an online learning platform might use real-time analytics to recommend additional resources or adjust lesson difficulty based on a student's performance. Universities and schools can also use real-time data to optimize resource allocation, such as scheduling classes and managing campus facilities.

Real-time analytics is a transformative technology that is reshaping industries and unlocking new possibilities for innovation and growth. From improving customer experiences to optimizing operations, its applications are as diverse as the industries it serves. By harnessing the power of real-time data, organizations can stay ahead of the curve, respond to challenges with agility, and create value for their stakeholders. Real-time analytics continues to evolve, pushing the boundaries of how industries operate and deliver value to their stakeholders. While we have explored several applications across various sectors, the potential for real-time analytics goes even deeper, especially as emerging technologies and methodologies redefine what is possible. This section will expand on the broader implications, niche use cases, and untapped potential of real-time analytics across different fields.

In agriculture, real-time analytics is revolutionizing traditional farming practices through precision agriculture. By integrating IoT sensors, drones, and satellite imagery, farmers can monitor soil health, crop conditions, and weather patterns in real time. For example, sensors embedded in the soil can provide live data on moisture levels, nutrient content, and temperature, allowing farmers to optimize irrigation and fertilization schedules. This not only reduces waste but also increases crop yields and minimizes environmental impact. Similarly, drones equipped with real-time imaging capabilities can identify pest infestations or diseases early, enabling targeted interventions that save resources and protect crops.

The aerospace and defense industry is another domain where real-time analytics is making a significant impact. In aviation, real-time data from aircraft sensors is used to monitor engine performance, predict maintenance needs, and enhance flight safety. Airlines can use this data to reduce delays, minimize unscheduled maintenance, and improve fuel efficiency. In defense, real-time analytics supports mission-critical operations by providing situational awareness, threat detection, and decision-making insights. For example, military drones rely on real-time analytics to process live video feeds, identify targets, and adapt to changing conditions during missions.

In the context of environmental conservation, real-time analytics is being used to address pressing global challenges such as climate change, deforestation, and wildlife preservation. Organizations and researchers are leveraging real-time data from satellites, sensors, and mobile devices to monitor ecosystems, track wildlife populations, and predict environmental changes. For instance, real-time analytics can help predict and mitigate the impact of natural disasters, such as hurricanes or wildfires, by analyzing weather data and environmental conditions. Conservationists can also use real-time data to track illegal activities, such as poaching or deforestation, and respond quickly to protect endangered species and habitats.

The insurance industry is undergoing a transformation driven by real-time analytics, particularly in areas like claims processing, risk assessment, and customer engagement. Insurers are using telematics devices in vehicles to collect real-time driving data, enabling usage-based insurance models that reward safe driving behaviors with lower premiums. Similarly, real-time analytics allows insurers to assess claims more accurately and efficiently by analyzing live data from incidents, such as photos, videos, or IoT sensors. This reduces fraud, speeds up claims' resolution, and improves customer satisfaction. Moreover, real-time analytics can help insurers predict and mitigate risks, such as identifying high-risk areas prone to natural disasters or accidents.

In the realm of education, real-time analytics is fostering more inclusive and effective learning environments. Beyond tracking individual student performance, educational institutions are using real-time data to identify trends and patterns across entire classrooms or schools. For example, real-time attendance tracking systems can identify patterns of absenteeism, enabling educators to intervene early and address underlying issues. Adaptive learning platforms powered by real-time analytics can adjust instructional content and pacing to suit the needs of diverse learners, ensuring no student is left behind. These insights empower educators to make data-driven decisions that enhance teaching effectiveness and student outcomes.

Real-time analytics is also proving invaluable in crisis management and humanitarian efforts. During emergencies, such as natural disasters, pandemics, or conflicts, real-time data is critical for coordinating responses and allocating resources efficiently. Organizations like the Red Cross and UN agencies rely on real-time analytics to track the movement of displaced populations, monitor supply chain logistics, and predict areas of greatest need. For example, during a flood, real-time analytics can identify regions at risk, optimize evacuation routes, and prioritize rescue operations. Similarly, in pandemic scenarios, real-time analytics can track infection rates, hospital capacity, and vaccination progress, enabling more effective public health interventions.

In the world of sports, real-time analytics is enhancing both player performance and fan engagement. Teams and coaches use live data from wearable devices, video analysis, and game statistics to monitor player fitness, develop strategies, and make in-game decisions. For instance, during a football match, real-time data on player positioning and stamina can guide substitutions or tactical adjustments. Meanwhile, fans benefit from real-time insights through interactive broadcasts, live statistics, and augmented reality experiences. These innovations are transforming sports into a more dynamic and data-driven field, offering value to players, coaches, and spectators alike.

Another area where real-time analytics is gaining traction is in urban planning and smart city initiatives. Cities around the world are using real-time data to optimize infrastructure, improve public services, and enhance the quality of life for residents. For example, real-time traffic analytics helps city planners identify congestion hotspots and implement solutions such as dynamic traffic signals or public transit adjustments. Smart utilities use real-time data to monitor energy consumption, detect leaks, and optimize resource allocation, reducing costs and environmental impact. Additionally, real-time analytics supports public safety efforts by enabling faster responses to emergencies, such as crimes, accidents, or natural disasters.

Finally, the potential for real-time analytics extends into personal wellness and lifestyle applications. Wearable devices, such as fitness trackers and smartwatches, provide individuals with real-time insights into their health and activity levels. These devices can monitor metrics like heart rate, sleep patterns, and calorie intake, helping users make informed decisions about their well-being. Real-time analytics also powers applications in mental health, such as apps that monitor stress levels or provide mindfulness exercises based on real-time feedback. By empowering individuals with live data about their bodies and minds, real-time analytics is fostering a culture of proactive health management.

The applications of real-time analytics are as diverse as they are transformative. From agriculture and education to aerospace and smart cities, real-time data is driving innovation, solving complex challenges, and creating new opportunities for growth and impact. These examples demonstrate the versatility and power of real-time analytics in reshaping industries and improving lives.

As emerging technologies continue to redefine industries, real-time analytics plays a pivotal role in unlocking their potential. In artificial intelligence (AI) and machine learning (ML), real-time analytics forms the foundation for many applications that rely on live data to drive automation and decision-making. For example, autonomous vehicles depend on real-time analytics to process data from cameras, sensors, and radar systems. These vehicles analyze their surroundings, identify obstacles, and make driving decisions in milliseconds. Without real-time data processing, the safe and efficient operation of autonomous systems would be impossible.

Similarly, real-time analytics powers augmented reality (AR) and virtual reality (VR) experiences by delivering live updates that adapt to user interactions. In AR applications, real-time data enables dynamic overlays that blend seamlessly with the physical environment, whether it's displaying information during a navigation session or enhancing gameplay in mobile AR games. VR environments, on the other hand, use real-time analytics to track user movements, optimize graphics rendering, and create immersive experiences. These technologies rely on the ability to process and deliver data instantaneously, highlighting the importance of real-time analytics in creating seamless, engaging user experiences.

Blockchain technology, often associated with cryptocurrencies, also benefits from real-time analytics. In decentralized finance (DeFi), real-time analytics provides traders and investors with live updates on market trends, transaction statuses, and portfolio performance. Additionally, blockchain networks use real-time data to monitor transaction validity and detect fraudulent activities. Smart contracts, which execute actions automatically when predefined conditions are met, rely on real-time analytics to verify input and ensure accuracy. This integration between blockchain and real-time analytics is paving the way for more secure and transparent digital ecosystems.

4.1 The Role of Real-Time Analytics in Sustainability and Climate Action

Real-time analytics is becoming a cornerstone of sustainability efforts and climate action initiatives. Organizations and governments are leveraging real-time data to monitor environmental conditions, optimize resource use, and reduce carbon footprints. For example, smart grids powered by real-time analytics enable utilities to manage energy distribution more efficiently, balancing supply and demand to minimize waste. Real-time data from sensors and IoT devices also helps track emissions, detect leaks in gas pipelines, and monitor air and water quality.

In agriculture, real-time analytics supports sustainable practices by providing farmers with precise insights into crop health and resource usage. By optimizing irrigation and fertilization schedules based on real-time soil data, farmers can conserve water and reduce the environmental impact of chemical runoff. Similarly, real-time weather analytics helps farmers anticipate extreme weather events, such as droughts or storms, and take proactive measures to protect their crops and livestock.

Real-time analytics is also instrumental in combating climate change by enabling early detection of environmental changes and disasters. Satellites equipped with real-time imaging capabilities monitor deforestation, glacier melting, and rising sea levels, providing critical data for researchers and policymakers. This live information helps governments and organizations respond swiftly to environmental crises, allocate resources effectively, and implement mitigation strategies. For instance, during a wildfire, real-time analytics can track the spread of flames and guide evacuation efforts, minimizing loss of life and property.

Furthermore, real-time analytics fosters a circular economy by enabling businesses to monitor waste streams and optimize recycling processes. Companies can use real-time data to track product lifecycles, identify inefficiencies, and design more sustainable supply chains. For example, manufacturers can analyze real-time data from production lines to minimize material waste and energy consumption, while retailers can use live inventory data to reduce overproduction and excess stock. These practices not only benefit the environment but also drive cost savings and operational efficiency.

4.2 Real-Time Analytics in Cultural and Creative Industries

Even in cultural and creative sectors, real-time analytics is proving to be a significant change. Museums and galleries are using real-time data to enhance visitor experiences by personalizing tours and optimizing exhibit layouts based on visitor preferences and behavior. For example, real-time analytics can track the movement of visitors within a museum, providing insights into which exhibits attract the most attention. This data allows curators to design more engaging layouts and allocate resources more effectively.

In the music industry, real-time analytics is helping artists and producers understand audience reactions and trends. Streaming platforms use live data to analyze listening habits, enabling musicians to tailor their releases and marketing strategies. During live performances, real-time analytics can track crowd engagement through social media interactions, ticket scans, and even wearable devices that measure audience excitement. These insights empower artists to create more memorable experiences and connect with their fans on a deeper level.

Film and television producers are also leveraging real-time analytics to make data-driven decisions during production and post-production. Streaming platforms like Netflix use real-time data to identify viewing patterns, optimize content recommendations, and even inform future programming decisions. Similarly, real-time analytics tools enable editors and directors to monitor audience responses to test screenings, making adjustments to improve a film's reception before its release.

In gaming, real-time analytics is reshaping the way developers create and refine games. Multiplayer online games rely on real-time data to match players with opponents of similar skill levels, ensuring fair and competitive gameplay. Developers also use real-time analytics to monitor server performance, identify technical issues, and balance game mechanics. Additionally, live feedback from players helps developers release timely updates and content, keeping games fresh and engaging.

By delving into emerging technologies, sustainability, and creative industries, it becomes evident that real-time analytics is far more versatile and impactful than often realized. Its applications are expanding into every aspect of modern life, offering solutions to challenges that range from environmental conservation to immersive entertainment. As we move forward, the potential for real-time analytics will only continue to grow, enabling industries and individuals to achieve unprecedented levels of innovation, efficiency, and creativity.

CHAPTER 5
Building High-Performance Real-Time Systems

The power of real-time analytics lies not just in its potential applications but in its underlying architecture. Building a high-performance real-time system is both an art and a science, requiring careful planning, robust design principles, and strategic execution. This chapter explores the technical and strategic considerations for designing, deploying, and managing real-time analytics systems that can deliver insights with speed, accuracy, and reliability.

At the heart of any high-performance real-time system is a well-designed data pipeline. The data pipeline is the backbone that enables the seamless flow of information from its source to its destination, where it is processed and analyzed. Designing a pipeline for real-time analytics requires balancing multiple factors, such as speed, scalability, fault tolerance, and cost efficiency. Each stage of the pipeline—data ingestion, processing, storage, and delivery—must be optimized to handle large volumes of data with minimal latency.

Data ingestion is the first and perhaps most critical stage of the pipeline. Real-time systems must collect data from diverse sources, including IoT sensors, application logs, social media platforms, and transactional systems. This data often arrives in different formats and at varying rates, requiring a flexible and scalable ingestion mechanism. Tools like Apache Kafka, Apache Pulsar, and Amazon Kinesis are widely used for their ability to handle high-throughput data streams with low latency. These tools ensure that data is captured reliably and made available for processing in real time.

The next stage in the pipeline is data processing, where raw data is transformed into actionable insights. Real-time processing frameworks like Apache Flink, Apache Spark Streaming, and Google Cloud Dataflow enable organizations to perform complex transformations, such as filtering, aggregating, and enriching data. These frameworks are designed to operate in distributed environments, allowing them to handle massive data volumes efficiently. A key consideration in this stage is latency, data must be processed quickly enough to provide actionable insights without compromising accuracy. Techniques like in-memory processing and parallel computation are often used to achieve this balance.

Data storage is another critical component of a high-performance real-time system. Unlike traditional batch processing systems that rely on relational databases, real-time analytics often requires specialized storage solutions that can handle high-speed read and write operations. NoSQL databases, such as MongoDB, Cassandra, and Amazon DynamoDB, are popular choices for their ability to store unstructured and semi-structured data. In-memory data stores like Redis and Memcached are also commonly used to reduce latency and improve query performance.

The final stage of the pipeline is data delivery, where processed insights are sent to their intended destinations. This could involve updating dashboards, triggering alerts, or feeding data into machine learning models for further analysis. Visualization tools like Tableau, Power BI, and Grafana play a crucial role in this stage, enabling users to interpret data and make informed decisions. Real-time alerting systems, such as PagerDuty or Splunk, ensure that critical insights reach the right stakeholders immediately, allowing for timely action.

Building a high-performance real-time system also requires robust architecture that can handle failures and disruptions. Fault tolerance is a key design principle, ensuring that the system can recover from hardware failures, network interruptions, or software bugs without losing data or compromising performance. Techniques like data replication, checkpointing, and distributed consensus algorithms are commonly used to achieve fault tolerance. For example, Apache Kafka's replication feature ensures that data is stored across multiple nodes, providing redundancy in case of node failure.

Scalability is another essential consideration. As organizations grow and their data volumes increase, real-time systems must be able to scale dynamically to meet demand. Horizontal scaling, which involves adding more nodes to the system, is often preferred over vertical scaling, which relies on upgrading individual nodes. Cloud platforms like AWS, Azure, and Google Cloud provide auto-scaling features that allow real-time systems to adjust resources automatically based on workload.

Latency optimization is a critical aspect of building high-performance systems. Even minor delays can render real-time insights obsolete, particularly in industries like finance or healthcare where split-second decisions are crucial. To minimize latency, organizations often use edge computing, which processes data closer to its source rather than relying on centralized servers. This approach reduces the time required for data to travel across networks, making it ideal for applications like autonomous vehicles or industrial IoT.

Security is another cornerstone of high-performance real-time systems. As data flows through multiple stages of the pipeline, it must be protected from unauthorized access, breaches, and tampering. Encryption, access controls, and real-time monitoring are essential for ensuring data security. Organizations must also comply with regulations like GDPR, CCPA, or HIPAA, particularly if they handle sensitive personal or financial information. Cloud providers often offer built-in security features, but organizations must implement additional measures to protect their specific use cases.

Cost management is an often-overlooked aspect of building real-time systems. While the pay-as-you-go model of cloud platforms provides financial flexibility, real-time analytics can become expensive if resources are not managed carefully. Organizations must monitor resource usage, optimize workflows, and eliminate redundancies to keep costs under control. For example, using serverless computing for event-driven analytics tasks can reduce costs by ensuring that resources are only used when needed.

Building a high-performance real-time system also requires collaboration across teams. Data engineers, data scientists, IT administrators, and business stakeholders must work together to define requirements, design workflows, and monitor performance. Agile methodologies, which emphasize iterative development and continuous feedback, are particularly well-suited to the dynamic nature of real-time analytics projects.

Finally, organizations must invest in monitoring and observability to ensure the ongoing performance of their real-time systems. Tools like Prometheus, ELK Stack, and Datadog provide real-time insights into system health, helping teams identify and resolve issues proactively. Observability goes beyond traditional monitoring by providing context about why an issue occurred, enabling faster and more effective troubleshooting.

Building a high-performance real-time system requires a holistic approach that considers technical, strategic, and operational factors. From designing efficient data pipelines to ensuring fault tolerance and security, every aspect of the system must be optimized for speed, accuracy, and reliability. By following best practices and leveraging the latest tools and technologies, organizations can unlock the full potential of real-time analytics and gain a competitive edge in their respective industries. Building a high-performance real-time system is not a one-time effort; it is an ongoing process that requires continuous monitoring, evaluation, and improvement. As data volumes grow and business requirements evolve, systems must be fine-tuned to maintain their performance and relevance. This involves regularly reviewing pipeline efficiency, updating algorithms, and adopting new technologies that enhance capabilities.

One critical aspect of continuous improvement is performance benchmarking. Organizations must establish clear metrics for measuring the performance of their real-time systems, such as latency, throughput, error rates, and resource utilization. These metrics provide a baseline for evaluating system health and identifying areas for optimization. For example, if a real-time pipeline experiences periodic spikes in latency, teams can investigate the root cause—whether it is network congestion, inefficient processing, or hardware limitations—and implement targeted solutions.

Automation plays a significant role in maintaining high-performance systems. Automated monitoring and alerting tools enable organizations to detect anomalies and address issues before they escalate. For example, an automated system might flag a sudden increase in dropped data packets, prompting engineers to investigate and resolve the problem. Automation also reduces the manual effort required to manage pipelines, allowing teams to focus on strategic improvements rather than routine maintenance.

Another strategy for optimization is workload partitioning, which involves dividing data into smaller, manageable chunks that can be processed independently. This approach, often implemented using techniques like sharding or partitioning, improves parallelism and reduces bottlenecks in the pipeline. For instance, a streaming platform processing user activity data might partition the data by geographic region, ensuring that no single server is overwhelmed with requests.

Regular system audits are also essential for maintaining high performance. These audits should evaluate not only technical performance but also alignment with business goals. For example, a system initially designed for fraud detection may need to evolve to accommodate new use cases, such as customer behavior analysis. By conducting periodic reviews, organizations can ensure their systems remain relevant and continue to deliver value. Emerging technologies are constantly reshaping the landscape of real-time analytics, offering new tools and techniques for building high-performance systems. One such technology is machine learning (ML), which is increasingly being integrated into real-time pipelines to enhance decision-making and automation. ML algorithms can be used to optimize system performance by predicting and addressing potential issues before they occur. For example, predictive models can identify patterns of system failure, enabling proactive maintenance and minimizing downtime.

Another promising technology is edge computing, which processes data closer to its source rather than relying on centralized servers. By reducing the distance data must travel, edge computing significantly lowers latency and enhances real-time system performance. This is particularly valuable for applications like autonomous vehicles, smart factories, and remote monitoring, where rapid decision-making is critical. For instance, an industrial IoT system using edge computing can analyze equipment performance in real time, detecting and resolving issues before they impact production.

Serverless computing is another innovation transforming real-time systems. By abstracting the underlying infrastructure, serverless platforms like AWS Lambda or Azure Functions allow developers to focus on building and deploying analytics workflows without worrying about managing servers. This approach simplifies system design, reduces operational overhead, and improves scalability. Serverless computing is particularly well-suited for event-driven tasks, such as processing user interactions or triggering alerts in response to specific conditions.

Quantum computing, though still in its early stages, holds immense potential for optimizing real-time systems. Quantum algorithms can solve complex optimization problems and process massive datasets at unprecedented speeds, making them ideal for use cases like supply chain management, financial modeling, and scientific simulations. As quantum computing becomes more accessible through cloud platforms, organizations will have new opportunities to enhance their real-time analytics capabilities.

The integration of artificial intelligence (AI) into real-time systems is another transformative trend. AI-powered analytics tools can automate complex tasks, such as anomaly detection, sentiment analysis, and natural language processing. For example, an e-commerce platform might use AI to analyze customer reviews in real time, identifying trends and addressing issues proactively. These capabilities not only improve system performance but also enable organizations to deliver more personalized and impactful experiences.

While the goal of building a high-performance real-time system is to maximize speed, accuracy, and reliability, achieving these objectives often involves trade-offs. Organizations must balance competing priorities, such as cost, complexity, and resource constraints, to design systems that meet their specific needs.

One common trade-off is between latency and accuracy. Reducing latency often requires simplifying algorithms or processing fewer data points, which can compromise the quality of insights. For example, a real-time recommendation system might prioritize speed over precision during peak usage periods, delivering "good enough" suggestions to maintain user satisfaction. Organizations must evaluate the importance of accuracy in different contexts and adjust their systems accordingly.

Another trade-off involves scalability and cost. While cloud platforms offer virtually unlimited scalability, excessive resource usage can lead to high costs. Organizations must monitor their cloud spending closely and implement cost-saving measures, such as optimizing workflows or using reserved instances. For instance, a logistics company might use serverless computing for real-time route optimization, scaling resources dynamically during peak delivery hours and minimizing costs during off-peak times.

Complexity is another factor to consider. High-performance systems often involve multiple components, tools, and integrations, which can increase the risk of errors and make troubleshooting more challenging. Simplifying system design and standardizing workflows can help reduce complexity without sacrificing performance. For example, adopting a microservices architecture allows teams to isolate and address issues in individual components, improving overall system reliability.

5. 1 Incorporating Observability and Monitoring for Sustained Performance

A crucial aspect of maintaining high-performance real-time systems is the integration of observability and monitoring tools. While monitoring focuses on tracking metrics like latency, throughput, and error rates, observability takes this step further by providing insights into the system's internal state, allowing teams to understand why issues occur. This distinction is critical for real-time systems, where rapid troubleshooting can mean the difference between seamless operations and significant disruptions.

To achieve effective observability, organizations must implement tools and frameworks that provide real-time visibility into the entire data pipeline. Solutions like Prometheus, Grafana, and the ELK Stack (Elasticsearch, Logstash, and Kibana) enable teams to monitor system performance in real time, visualize key metrics, and analyze logs for anomalies. For instance, if a sudden spike in latency is detected, these tools can help pinpoint the exact stage in the pipeline causing the delay, such as a bottleneck in data ingestion or an overloaded processing node.

Distributed tracing is another critical component of observability in high-performance systems. By tracking the journey of individual data packets through the pipeline, tracing tools like Jaeger or Open Telemetry provide a detailed view of how requests are processed, where delays occur, and how different components interact. This level of insight is invaluable for debugging complex systems with multiple dependencies.

Proactive alerting mechanisms are also essential for maintaining system health. Tools like PagerDuty or Splunk can be configured to send real-time alerts when performance metrics exceed predefined thresholds, such as high error rates or low resource availability. These alerts enable teams to respond to issues before they escalate, minimizing downtime and ensuring consistent performance.

Furthermore, observability frameworks should integrate with incident response workflows to streamline resolution processes. For example, when an alert is triggered, it can automatically create a ticket in a project management tool, assign it to the appropriate team, and provide detailed diagnostic information. This reduces the time needed to identify and fix issues, enhancing overall system reliability.

5.2 Future-Proofing Real-Time Systems: Trends and Best Practices

The rapid pace of technological advancements means that today's high-performance real-time systems must be designed with the future in mind. Future-proofing these systems involves adopting flexible architectures, staying ahead of emerging trends, and building resilience against potential challenges.

One of the most promising trends in real-time analytics is the rise of event-driven architectures. Unlike traditional request-response models, event-driven systems process data as events occur, enabling faster and more efficient workflows. For example, an e-commerce platform might use an event-driven architecture to automatically update inventory levels and send alerts when stock runs low. By embracing this approach, organizations can build systems that are more responsive and adaptable to changing conditions.

Another emerging trend is the use of real-time analytics at the edge. As IoT devices become more prevalent, the need for localized data processing is growing. Edge computing allows organizations to process data closer to its source, reducing latency and bandwidth usage. For example, a smart city might use edge analytics to process traffic data in real time, enabling dynamic adjustments to traffic lights and improving urban mobility. Integrating edge computing with centralized cloud systems ensures that real-time analytics can scale to meet the demands of increasingly connected environments.

Artificial intelligence (AI) and machine learning (ML) are also shaping the future of real-time systems. These technologies enable predictive and prescriptive analytics, where systems can anticipate issues and recommend solutions. For example, a logistics company might use ML models to predict delivery delays based on real-time traffic data, weather conditions, and historical trends. By integrating AI and ML into real-time systems, organizations can move beyond reactive decision-making to proactive and even autonomous operations.

Resilience is another critical factor in future-proofing real-time systems. Cybersecurity threats, natural disasters, and technical failures can disrupt operations, making it essential to build systems that can withstand and recover from these challenges. Strategies like data redundancy, distributed architectures, and regular disaster recovery drills help ensure that real-time systems remain operational under adverse conditions. For example, a financial institution might replicate its real-time data across multiple data centers to protect against localized outages and ensure uninterrupted service.

Finally, staying informed about regulatory changes and industry standards is essential for future-proofing real-time systems. As data privacy and security regulations continue to evolve, organizations must ensure that their systems comply with requirements like GDPR, CCPA, or sector-specific guidelines. This involves implementing robust data governance policies, conducting regular compliance audits, and adapting systems to meet new requirements as they emerge.

High-performance real-time systems are the engine of modern analytics, enabling organizations to harness the full potential of their data. By incorporating observability and monitoring, leveraging emerging technologies, and adopting future-proofing strategies, businesses can build systems that are not only efficient but also resilient and adaptable. These systems empower organizations to make faster, smarter decisions, driving innovation and delivering value in an increasingly data-driven world.

CHAPTER 6
Real-Time Visualization and Reporting

While high-performance real-time systems generate a wealth of valuable data, their effectiveness hinges on how well these insights are communicated to stakeholders. Real-time visualization and reporting serve as the bridge between raw analytics and actionable decisions. This chapter explores the principles, tools, and strategies that enable organizations to present real-time data in ways that drive clarity, engagement, and impact.

Real-time visualization is not just about displaying data, it is about telling a story that empowers decision-makers to act quickly and confidently. The human brain processes visual information faster than text or numbers, making well-designed visualizations a powerful tool for interpreting complex data sets. In a business setting, real-time dashboards can provide executives with an at-a-glance overview of key performance indicators (KPIs), helping them identify trends, monitor progress, and respond to emerging challenges.

The design of real-time dashboards and reports is critical to their effectiveness. A well-designed dashboard should prioritize clarity, relevance, and simplicity, presenting information in a way that is both intuitive and actionable. For example, a sales dashboard might use color-coded metrics to highlight regions with declining revenue, while a logistics dashboard might display live maps with traffic overlays to help optimize delivery routes. Visual elements like graphs, charts, and heat maps can make patterns and outliers more apparent, enabling users to draw insights at a glance.

Interactivity is another key feature of effective real-time visualizations. Interactive dashboards allow users to drill down into specific data points, customize views, and explore underlying details. For instance, a marketing team analyzing campaign performance might use a dashboard to filter results by region, demographic, or time period, uncovering insights that inform future strategies. This level of interactivity not only enhances user engagement but also encourages deeper exploration and understanding of the data.

Real-time reporting complements visualizations by providing detailed summaries and narratives that contextualize the data. Unlike static reports, which are typically generated on a periodic basis, real-time reports are dynamic and continuously updated as new data becomes available. These reports are often used for operational decision-making, such as monitoring production lines, tracking customer service metrics, or evaluating financial performance. Automated reporting tools can generate and distribute real-time updates to relevant stakeholders, ensuring that everyone has access to the latest information.

To achieve effective real-time visualization and reporting, organizations must choose the right tools and platforms. Popular visualization tools like Tableau, Power BI, and Grafana offer robust features for creating interactive dashboards and reports. These tools integrate seamlessly with real-time data sources, allowing users to visualize and analyze live information with ease. Additionally, open-source frameworks like D3.js and Plotly provide flexible options for creating custom visualizations tailored to specific use cases.

Real-time alerting systems play a crucial role in complementing visualization and reporting efforts. Alerts provide immediate notifications when certain thresholds or conditions are met, enabling proactive responses to critical events. For example, a security team might receive an alert when unusual activity is detected in a network, while a healthcare provider might be notified when a patient's vitals fall outside safe ranges. By combining real-time visualizations with targeted alerts, organizations can ensure that stakeholders stay informed and can act swiftly when needed.

The effectiveness of real-time visualizations also depends on the quality and accuracy of the underlying data. Data inaccuracies or inconsistencies can lead to misleading insights, undermining trust in the system and resulting in poor decision-making. Organizations must implement data validation processes and ensure that their pipelines are optimized for accuracy and reliability. For example, using real-time data quality checks to identify anomalies or discrepancies before they reach the dashboard can help maintain the integrity of visualizations.

Personalization is an emerging trend in real-time visualization and reporting. Tailored dashboards and reports that cater to the specific needs of individual users or teams can enhance engagement and utility. For instance, a finance team might require detailed charts on budget allocation and expenses, while a marketing team might focus on lead generation and conversion metrics. Personalization ensures that users receive the most relevant insights, reducing information overload and improving decision-making efficiency.

Mobile accessibility is another critical consideration in today's fast-paced business environment. Decision-makers are increasingly relying on smartphones and tablets to access real-time insights on the go. Visualization and reporting tools must be designed with responsive layouts and mobile-friendly interfaces to ensure seamless access across devices. For example, a mobile-optimized dashboard for a logistics manager might display key metrics like delivery status, driver locations, and estimated arrival times in a compact and easily navigable format.

Despite its many advantages, real-time visualization and reporting come with challenges. One of the most significant is ensuring that visualizations remain actionable and not overwhelming. The temptation to include too much data or overly complex visuals can dilute the effectiveness of the dashboard, leading to confusion rather than clarity. Organizations must strike a balance between providing comprehensive information and maintaining simplicity.

Another challenge is maintaining real-time performance. As data volumes grow, ensuring that visualizations update in real time without delays can become increasingly difficult. Tools and platforms must be optimized to handle high-speed data streams, and infrastructure must be scaled appropriately to meet demand. Techniques like catching frequently accessed data and using in-memory databases can help improve performance and reduce latency.

Organizations must address the issue of data security and privacy in real-time visualization and reporting. Dashboards and reports often contain sensitive information, making them a potential target for cyberattacks. Implementing robust access controls, encryption, and monitoring is essential to protect data and maintain user trust.

The integration of artificial intelligence (AI) and machine learning (ML) into real-time visualization and reporting is an exciting development that is transforming how insights are presented and utilized. Predictive analytics, powered by AI, enables dashboards to go beyond descriptive metrics and provide foresight into future trends and events. For example, a sales dashboard might use predictive models to forecast revenue based on current performance, allowing teams to adjust their strategies proactively.

AI-powered recommendations are another innovation enhancing real-time visualizations. These systems analyze data patterns and suggest actions to optimize outcomes. For instance, a marketing dashboard might recommend reallocating budget to high-performing campaigns, while a supply chain dashboard might suggest rerouting shipments to avoid delays. These intelligent features not only enhance the utility of dashboards but also empower users to make data-driven decisions with confidence.

Natural language processing (NLP) is also making real-time reporting more accessible. With NLP, users can interact with dashboards and reports using plain language queries, such as "Show me sales trends for the last quarter" or "Which regions have the highest customer churn?" This capability simplifies data exploration and ensures that insights are accessible even to non-technical users.

Real-time visualization and reporting are the linchpins of effective real-time analytics, transforming raw data into actionable insights that drive better decisions. By prioritizing clarity, interactivity, and personalization, organizations can create dashboards and reports that empower stakeholders at all levels. As technologies like AI and NLP continue to advance, the possibilities for real-time visualization and reporting will only grow, enabling more intuitive and impactful ways to engage with data.

An emerging frontier in real-time visualization and reporting is the development of contextual and adaptive dashboards. These dashboards dynamically adjust their content and layout based on the user's role, preferences, and current context. By delivering insights tailored to specific use cases, contextual dashboards reduce cognitive load and enable users to focus on the most relevant data.

For example, in a logistics company, a warehouse manager might need real-time updates on inventory levels and order statuses, while a delivery driver may require live route optimizations and traffic conditions. Contextual dashboards automatically display the appropriate information based on the user's role and location, ensuring that every stakeholder gets the insights they need without wading through irrelevant data.

Adaptive dashboards go a step further by adjusting to changes in real-time conditions. These systems use algorithms to prioritize critical information during high-pressure situations. For instance, in an IT operations center, an adaptive dashboard might suppress non-urgent metrics during a system outage and highlight alerts, root cause analyses, and mitigation steps instead. Once the crisis is resolved, the dashboard can revert to its default state, resuming regular monitoring activities.

Such adaptability is made possible by integrating machine learning into the visualization layer. By analyzing user behavior and historical interactions, machine learning models can predict what information a user is likely to need at any given moment and adjust the dashboard accordingly. This approach ensures that users are always equipped with the most actionable insights, enhancing their efficiency and decision-making capabilities.

Real-time visualizations are not just tools for individual decision-making; they are powerful enablers of collaboration across teams and departments. When shared effectively, real-time dashboards and reports can align stakeholders around common goals, facilitate discussions, and drive consensus on critical issues.

One way to foster collaboration is by integrating real-time dashboards with communication and project management platforms. For example, linking dashboards to tools like Microsoft Teams, Slack, or Asana allows teams to discuss insights, assign tasks, and track progress directly within their workflows. A marketing team reviewing campaign performance in real time could use integrated dashboards to highlight areas of improvement and immediately assign follow-up actions, ensuring that insights translate into tangible outcomes.

Shared dashboards are also valuable for fostering transparency and accountability within organizations. By making real-time data accessible to all relevant stakeholders, shared dashboards create a culture of data-driven decision-making. For example, a retail company might provide its regional managers with access to a live sales dashboard, enabling them to compare performance across locations and share the best practices. This approach not only improves individual performance but also strengthens the organization's overall alignment and execution.

Another critical feature for collaborative decision-making is annotation and storytelling within dashboards. Tools that allow users to annotate data points, add context, or highlight trends make it easier to communicate insights effectively. For instance, a sales manager preparing a quarterly performance review might annotate key milestones and challenges on a revenue trend chart, providing the executive team with a clear narrative that supports strategic planning.

Interactive reporting also plays a significant role in collaborative decision-making. By enabling multiple stakeholders to explore data simultaneously and customize views, interactive reports facilitate deeper discussions and more informed decisions. For example, during a supply chain review meeting, team members could explore real-time metrics on delays, costs, and inventory levels, identifying bottlenecks and collectively devising solutions.

As visualization technologies evolve, augmented reality (AR) and virtual reality (VR) are emerging as transformative tools for presenting real-time data. These immersive technologies enable users to interact with data in three-dimensional spaces, offering new ways to explore and understand complex information.

In AR applications, real-time data can be overlaid onto physical environments, enhancing situational awareness and decision-making. For example, an operations manager at a factory might use AR glasses to view live production metrics overlaid onto machinery, identifying inefficiencies or maintenance needs at a glance. Similarly, in healthcare, AR can provide surgeons with real-time patient data, such as vitals and imaging, during procedures, improving precision and outcomes.

VR takes this a step further by creating fully immersive environments where users can explore data in ways that are not possible with traditional screens. For instance, a team analyzing a city's traffic patterns might use VR to visualize data as a 3D model, allowing them to identify congestion hotspots and test the impact of proposed changes in a simulated environment. This level of interactivity and immersion fosters deeper understanding and enables more innovative problem-solving.

As AR and VR technologies become more accessible, they are likely to play an increasingly significant role in real-time analytics, particularly in industries where spatial context and complex data visualization are critical.

Despite their many advantages, real-time visualization and reporting systems face several challenges that organizations must address to maximize their effectiveness. One of the most common issues is data overload. With the ability to process vast amounts of data in real time, there is a risk of overwhelming users with too much information. To mitigate this, organizations should adopt a "less is more" approach, focusing on the most critical metrics and using hierarchical layouts to present data in digestible chunks.

Another challenge is ensuring that visualizations remain inclusive and accessible to all users. Dashboards and reports must be designed with accessibility in mind, including features like adjustable font sizes, high-contrast color schemes, and screen reader compatibility. These considerations ensure that insights are accessible to users with diverse abilities and preferences.

Latency in real-time visualization is another significant hurdle, especially as data volumes grow. Even minor delays can undermine the utility of real-time dashboards, particularly in scenarios where immediate action is required. Organizations must invest in optimized infrastructure, including in-memory databases, efficient query engines, and scalable cloud platforms, to maintain real-time performance.

Organizations must address the cultural challenges associated with adopting real-time visualization and reporting. Transitioning to a data-driven culture requires buy-in from leadership and training for employees to interpret and act on real-time insights. Without this cultural alignment, even the most advanced visualization tools may fail to deliver their full potential.

Driving Innovation with Advanced Visual Analytics

As real-time visualization evolves, advanced visual analytics techniques are enabling organizations to uncover deeper insights and drive innovation. Visual analytics combines the strengths of automated data analysis with human intuition, empowering users to interact with data in meaningful ways. Through the use of advanced techniques like geospatial analysis, temporal analysis, and network analysis, organizations can extract valuable patterns and connections that traditional methods might overlook.

Geospatial analysis is particularly transformative for industries that rely on location-based data, such as logistics, urban planning, and retail. By visualizing real-time data on maps, organizations can track assets, monitor regional trends, and optimize operations. For example, a logistics company might use geospatial dashboards to monitor vehicle locations, delivery routes, and traffic conditions in real time, ensuring timely deliveries and efficient fleet management. Similarly, a retail chain could analyze foot traffic patterns to determine the best locations for new stores or promotional campaigns.

Temporal analysis, which focuses on changes and trends over time, is another powerful tool in visual analytics. Real-time dashboards that incorporate temporal components, such as animated graphs or time-lapse visualizations, allow users to identify patterns and anomalies as they develop. For instance, an energy company monitoring grid performance might use temporal analysis to detect spikes in electricity consumption, enabling rapid adjustments to prevent outages. Temporal visualizations also play a critical role in fraud detection, where identifying unusual sequences of events in real time can help prevent financial losses.

Network analysis, which visualizes relationships and connections between data points, is increasingly being used in cybersecurity, telecommunications, and social network analysis. Real-time network diagrams can reveal hidden connections, bottlenecks, and vulnerabilities within complex systems. For example, a cybersecurity team might use network analysis to monitor real-time traffic flows and identify suspicious activity, such as unauthorized access attempts or distributed denial-of-service (DDoS) attacks. These insights enable proactive responses to potential threats, reducing the risk of security breaches.

6.1 The Future of Real-Time Visualization: Augmenting Intelligence with AI

As artificial intelligence (AI) becomes more integrated into real-time analytics, its role in visualization is evolving from enhancing user experiences to augmenting human intelligence. AI-powered visualizations not only present data but also interpret it, providing users with recommendations, automated insights, and predictive trends. These capabilities are revolutionizing how decision-makers interact with real-time analytics.

One area where AI is transforming visualization is in anomaly detection. Traditional dashboards often require users to monitor metrics manually and identify anomalies based on their expertise. AI automates this process by continuously analyzing data streams and flagging deviations from expected patterns. For instance, an AI-enhanced sales dashboard might alert users to a sudden drop in revenue from a specific region, along with potential causes and recommended actions. This level of automation allows users to focus on strategic decision-making rather than data monitoring.

Another innovation is the use of AI to personalize visualizations. Machine learning models analyze user behavior and preferences to customize dashboards for individual needs. For example, a financial analyst tracking portfolio performance might receive a dashboard tailored to their specific investment strategies, highlighting metrics like risk exposure, sector performance, and dividend yields. This personalization reduces information overload and ensures that users can quickly access the insights most relevant to their roles.

Natural language generation (NLG) is also enhancing real-time reporting by automatically generating narrative explanations for complex data. Dashboards equipped with NLG capabilities can accompany visualizations with plain-language summaries, making insights accessible to non-technical users. For example, a healthcare dashboard monitoring hospital performance might include an automatically generated report stating, "Patient wait times increased by 10% in the last 24 hours, driven by higher-than-average admissions in the emergency department." These summaries simplify data interpretation and improve communication across teams.

AI is also driving innovation in predictive and prescriptive visualizations. Predictive visualizations leverage historical and real-time data to forecast future trends, enabling organizations to prepare for upcoming challenges and opportunities. For example, a retail dashboard might predict inventory shortages based on current sales trends and recommend restocking strategies to avoid disruptions. Prescriptive visualizations take this a step further by offering actionable recommendations, such as adjusting pricing, reallocating resources, or launching targeted marketing campaigns.

6.2 Integrating Real-Time Visualizations into Emerging Workflows

The future of real-time visualization lies in its seamless integration into workflows across industries. As remote work and hybrid teams become the norm, real-time dashboards and reports must adapt to new ways of working, enabling collaboration and decision-making across distributed teams.

One way to achieve this integration is through the use of embedded analytics. Instead of requiring users to access separate tools for visualization, embedded analytics integrates real-time dashboards directly into existing applications and platforms. For example, a CRM system with embedded real-time analytics might display sales trends and customer engagement metrics within the user interface, eliminating the need for users to switch between multiple tools. This integration streamlines workflows and ensures that insights are readily available when and where they are needed.

Another key trend is the rise of conversational analytics, which allows users to interact with real-time visualizations through natural language queries. Voice assistants and chatbots powered by AI enable users to ask questions like, "What's the current revenue in Region A?" or "Show me the top-performing products this month," and receive instant visual responses. This capability democratizes access to analytics, making real-time insights accessible to non-technical users and fostering a data-driven culture across the organization.

Mobile-first visualization is also gaining traction as organizations recognize the need for real-time insights on the go. Dashboards designed for mobile devices prioritize simplicity, responsiveness, and clarity, ensuring that users can access critical metrics even in high-pressure situations. For example, a field service manager might use a mobile dashboard to track technician locations and job statuses in real time, enabling efficient resource allocation and faster issue resolution.

Lastly, the integration of real-time visualizations with augmented and virtual reality (AR/VR) technologies is opening up new possibilities for immersive data exploration. For instance, a construction project manager might use AR glasses to overlay real-time progress metrics onto a physical site, while an urban planner could use VR to simulate the impact of proposed infrastructure changes. These technologies enable users to interact with data in innovative ways, fostering deeper insights and more informed decision-making.

OLUSHOLA IBRAHIM

CHAPTER 7
Security and Privacy in Real-Time Analytics

As organizations increasingly rely on real-time analytics to drive decisions, the importance of securing these systems cannot be overstated. Real-time analytics involves the continuous flow, processing, and storage of sensitive data, often in high volumes. Whether it is customer information, financial transactions, or operational metrics, this data must be safeguarded against breaches, misuse, and regulatory non-compliance. This chapter explores the challenges, strategies, and tools for ensuring the security and privacy of real-time analytics systems.

Real-time analytics systems are particularly vulnerable to security threats due to their always-on nature and reliance on distributed architectures. These systems often integrate data from multiple sources, including IoT devices, cloud platforms, and external APIs, creating numerous potential entry points for attackers. Cybersecurity risks, such as unauthorized access, data breaches, and distributed denial-of-service (DDoS) attacks, can disrupt real-time pipelines, compromise sensitive information, and erode user trust.

One of the foundational principles of securing real-time analytics is implementing a **zero-trust security model**. This approach assumes that no user, device, or application can be trusted by default, even if they are inside the network perimeter. Zero-trust security requires continuous verification of all access requests, using techniques such as multi-factor authentication (MFA), identity and access management (IAM), and behavioral analysis. For example, a real-time dashboard for monitoring financial transactions might require users to authenticate their identities via MFA every time they log in, ensuring that only authorized personnel can access sensitive data.

Encryption is another cornerstone of real-time analytics security. By encrypting data both in transit and at rest, organizations can protect sensitive information from interception or theft. Secure protocols like HTTPS and TLS should be used for data transmission, while strong encryption algorithms, such as AES-256, can safeguard stored data. For example, an e-commerce platform processing real-time payment data might encrypt all transaction details before storing them in a database, ensuring that even if the database is compromised, the data remains unreadable without the encryption key.

Data masking and anonymization are essential for protecting user privacy in real-time analytics. These techniques involve obscuring sensitive information, such as names, addresses, and payment details, while retaining its usability for analysis. For instance, a healthcare provider analyzing real-time patient data might replace personally identifiable information (PII) with pseudonyms or hashed values, ensuring that the data cannot be traced back to individuals. Anonymization is particularly important for organizations subject to privacy regulations, such as the General Data Protection Regulation (GDPR) or the California Consumer Privacy Act (CCPA).

Real-time analytics systems must also be designed with **role-based access control (RBAC)** to limit access to sensitive data based on users' roles and responsibilities. RBAC ensures that users can only view or manipulate the data they are authorized to access. For example, in a logistics company, a delivery driver might only have access to route data relevant to their assignments, while a manager can view performance metrics for the entire fleet. By enforcing the principle of least privilege, RBAC minimizes the risk of accidental or intentional data exposure.

Monitoring and auditing are critical for detecting and responding to security incidents in real time. Advanced threat detection tools, such as Security Information and Event Management (SIEM) systems, can analyze data from logs, network traffic, and user activity to identify suspicious behavior. For example, if a user attempts to download an unusually large volume of data from a real-time analytics dashboard, the SIEM system can trigger an alert, allowing security teams to investigate and mitigate potential threats. Regular audits of access logs and system configurations further enhance security by identifying vulnerabilities and ensuring compliance with best practices.

Compliance with data privacy and security regulations is a key consideration for organizations using real-time analytics. Laws like GDPR, CCPA, and HIPAA impose strict requirements on how data is collected, processed, stored, and shared, with significant penalties for non-compliance. Real-time systems must be designed to meet these requirements without compromising performance or user experience.

One of the challenges of achieving compliance in real-time analytics is managing **data sovereignty**. Many regulations require that data be stored and processed within specific geographic regions. For example, GDPR mandates that personal data of European Union residents must remain within the EU unless equivalent protections are guaranteed elsewhere. Organizations using real-time analytics must ensure that their systems are configured to comply with these requirements, often by selecting cloud providers with region-specific data centers.

Another compliance challenge is ensuring that data subject rights, such as the right to access, correct, or delete personal data, are respected in real-time systems. For instance, if a customer requests that their data be deleted, the organization must ensure that the deletion is propagated across all components of the real-time pipeline, including data sources, processing frameworks, and storage systems. Implementing automated workflows for handling such requests can streamline compliance and reduce the risk of errors.

To maintain compliance, organizations must also implement **privacy-by-design principles**, embedding privacy considerations into every stage of the real-time analytics lifecycle. This includes conducting data protection impact assessments (DPIAs) to evaluate the risks associated with data processing activities and implementing measures to mitigate those risks. For example, an organization deploying a real-time marketing dashboard might assess how user tracking affects privacy and take steps to minimize data collection while still achieving marketing goals.

As cyber threats become more sophisticated, organizations must adopt a proactive approach to securing their real-time analytics systems. Resilience is not just about preventing attacks but also about detecting, responding to, and recovering from incidents effectively.

Intrusion detection and prevention systems (IDPS) are essential for identifying and blocking unauthorized access to real-time pipelines. These systems use machine learning and behavioral analysis to detect anomalies, such as unusual login patterns or unexpected data flows. For example, an IDPS monitoring a real-time fraud detection system might flag an attacker attempting to inject malicious code into the pipeline.

Regular **penetration testing** is another key strategy for building resilience. By simulating cyberattacks, organizations can identify vulnerabilities in their real-time analytics systems and address them before they are exploited. For example, a financial institution might hire ethical hackers to test the security of its real-time transaction monitoring system, ensuring that it can withstand sophisticated attacks.

Disaster recovery planning is critical for minimizing downtime and data loss during security incidents. Real-time analytics systems should be equipped with backup and failover mechanisms, such as redundant data pipelines and geographically distributed storage. For instance, a healthcare provider using real-time patient monitoring might replicate its data across multiple regions, ensuring that vital information remains accessible even if one data center goes offline.

Securing and protecting the privacy of real-time analytics systems is a multifaceted challenge that requires a combination of advanced technologies, robust processes, and a proactive mindset. By implementing zero-trust security, encryption, role-based access controls, and compliance measures, organizations can safeguard sensitive data and maintain trust with their stakeholders. Additionally, building resilience through monitoring, penetration testing, and disaster recovery planning ensures that real-time systems remain operational even in the face of evolving cyber threats.

Artificial intelligence (AI) and automation emerging as significant changes in securing real-time analytics systems. These technologies enable organizations to detect and mitigate threats in real time, reducing the response time to potential breaches and improving overall system resilience. AI-driven security tools analyze vast amounts of data to identify patterns and anomalies that human analysts might miss, while automation streamlines the execution of security protocols to minimize human error.

For instance, AI-powered anomaly detection systems can continuously monitor real-time data pipelines for unusual behavior, such as unauthorized access attempts, unexpected data flows, or irregular traffic patterns. These systems use machine learning algorithms to establish baseline behaviors for users and systems, flagging deviations as potential threats. For example, if an employee account is accessed from an unfamiliar location and subsequently downloads large volumes of sensitive data, an AI system could immediately flag the activity and trigger an automated response, such as disabling the account or alerting the security team.

Automation also plays a critical role in incident response. By integrating real-time analytics systems with Security Orchestration, Automation, and Response (SOAR) platforms, organizations can automate the containment and mitigation of threats. For example, if a DDoS attack is detected, a SOAR platform could automatically reroute traffic, block malicious IP addresses, and activate backup servers to maintain system availability. This level of automation reduces the time between threat detection and response, minimizing damage and ensuring business continuity.

Additionally, AI enhances the security of real-time analytics systems through predictive analytics. By analyzing historical and real-time data, predictive models can identify trends and vulnerabilities, enabling organizations to proactively address risks before they escalate. For instance, a financial institution using predictive security analytics might identify patterns of fraudulent transactions that precede larger cyberattacks, allowing them to implement preventive measures in advance.

The rise of IoT and edge computing presents unique challenges and opportunities for securing real-time analytics systems. IoT devices generate vast amounts of data in real time, often processed at the edge to reduce latency and bandwidth usage. While this decentralized approach improves efficiency, it also creates additional attack surfaces that must be secured.

One of the primary concerns in IoT security is the vulnerability of devices themselves. Many IoT devices lack robust security features, making them susceptible to hacking. Securing IoT-driven real-time analytics systems requires implementing device authentication, ensuring that only authorized devices can send data to the pipeline. For example, a smart manufacturing facility might use digital certificates to verify the identity of sensors and machinery before allowing them to contribute data to the real-time analytics system.

Edge computing introduces further complexities by distributing data processing across multiple locations. This decentralized architecture necessitates securing data at each point of processing, as well as during transmission between the edge and the central cloud or data center. Encryption and secure communication protocols, such as MQTT and CoAP, are essential for protecting data in transit. For example, an edge-based traffic management system might encrypt vehicle location data as it is transmitted to a central dashboard, ensuring that sensitive information remains secure.

Another key strategy for securing IoT and edge systems is implementing edge-based security analytics. These solutions analyze data locally at the edge, identifying potential threats before they reach the central system. For instance, an industrial IoT system monitoring equipment performance might use edge-based anomaly detection to identify and isolate compromised devices, preventing them from disrupting the entire network.

While the technical aspects of securing real-time analytics systems are critical, organizations must also address the ethical considerations associated with data privacy and security. The collection and processing of real-time data often involve sensitive personal information, raising concerns about how this data is used and protected.

One ethical challenge is balancing security with user privacy. Implementing robust security measures, such as continuous monitoring and behavioral analytics, can sometimes feel intrusive to users. Organizations must ensure that their security practices are transparent, clearly communicate how data is collected and used, and provide users with control over their information. For example, a retail platform using real-time analytics to personalize recommendations might offer customers the ability to opt out of data tracking while still accessing basic services.

Another ethical concern is the potential for bias in AI-driven security systems. Machine learning models are only as good as the data they are trained on, and biased data can lead to unfair or discriminatory outcomes. For instance, an AI system designed to flag suspicious behavior might disproportionately target certain groups based on historical biases in the data. To address this, organizations must rigorously test their models for fairness and ensure that diverse perspectives are considered during development.

Data minimization is a critical principle for addressing ethical concerns in real-time analytics. Organizations should collect and process only the data that is strictly necessary for their operations, reducing the risk of misuse or unauthorized access. For example, a transportation company using real-time analytics to optimize routes might only collect aggregated location data rather than detailed trip histories, preserving user privacy while achieving operational goals.

Securing real-time analytics systems is not solely the responsibility of IT and security teams require a culture of security awareness across the entire organization. Employees at all levels must understand the importance of data security and their role in protecting sensitive information.

Regular training and awareness programs are essential for fostering this culture. These programs should educate employees on best practices, such as recognizing phishing attempts, creating strong passwords, and adhering to access control policies. For example, a company using real-time analytics for customer service might train its agents to identify social engineering attacks aimed at gaining access to customer data.

Leadership plays a critical role in reinforcing the importance of security. By prioritizing security initiatives, allocating resources, and leading by example, leaders can set the tone for the organization and ensure that security remains a top priority. For instance, a C-suite executive might sponsor an organization-wide security campaign, highlighting the value of protecting real-time analytics systems and the potential consequences of neglecting security.

Organizations can also encourage collaboration between teams to address security challenges holistically. Cross-functional security committees that include representatives from IT, legal, compliance, and operations can ensure that security strategies align with business objectives and regulatory requirements. For example, a healthcare provider implementing a real-time patient monitoring system might involve clinicians, data scientists, and compliance officers in the design process to balance security, functionality, and regulatory compliance.

The security and privacy of real-time analytics systems are integral to their success and trustworthiness. By leveraging advanced technologies like AI and automation, securing IoT and edge environments, and addressing ethical considerations, organizations can build robust systems that protect sensitive data while enabling real-time insights. Creating a culture of security awareness further reinforces these efforts, ensuring that every member of the organization contributes to safeguarding critical systems.

A critical, often overlooked aspect of securing real-time analytics systems is the integration of **threat intelligence**. Threat intelligence refers to the collection, analysis, and application of information about potential cyber threats and vulnerabilities. Incorporating real-time threat intelligence into analytics systems allows organizations to anticipate and proactively address emerging risks.

For example, a financial institution using real-time analytics for fraud detection might integrate threat intelligence feeds to monitor new tactics used by cybercriminals, such as phishing schemes or malware targeting payment systems. This information can be used to update anomaly detection models, ensuring that the system remains effective against evolving threats. Similarly, an e-commerce platform might use threat intelligence to identify and block IP addresses associated with botnets, reducing the risk of account takeovers and fake transactions.

Threat intelligence can also enhance the efficiency of Security Information and Event Management (SIEM) systems by providing context for alerts. For instance, if a SIEM system detects unusual activity in a real-time pipeline, threat intelligence can help determine whether the activity is linked to known attack patterns or is indicative of a new threat. This contextual information enables security teams to prioritize their responses, focusing on the most critical incidents.

To maximize the value of threat intelligence, organizations should leverage both external and internal sources. External sources include commercial and open-source threat intelligence feeds, industry-specific information-sharing platforms, and government advisories. Internal sources, such as logs from real-time analytics systems, can provide valuable insights into attack patterns specific to the organization. Combining these sources creates a more comprehensive view of the threat landscape, improving the organization's ability to detect and respond to cyber risks.

7.1 Leveraging Blockchain for Data Integrity and Security

Blockchain technology is emerging as a powerful tool for enhancing the security and integrity of real-time analytics systems. By providing a decentralized, tamper-proof ledger, blockchain ensures that data remains trustworthy and traceable throughout its lifecycle. This capability is particularly valuable for real-time systems that handle sensitive or high-stakes data, such as financial transactions, supply chain monitoring, or patient records.

One of the key benefits of blockchain is its ability to create immutable audit trails. In a real-time analytics context, every data transaction can be recorded as a block in the chain, complete with a timestamp and cryptographic hash. This makes it virtually impossible for attackers to alter historical data without detection. For example, in a logistics company using real-time analytics to track shipments, blockchain can verify that location data has not been tampered with, ensuring transparency and accountability.

Blockchain also enhances identity and access management in real-time systems. Decentralized identifiers (DIDs) stored on a blockchain enable secure, verifiable digital identities for users and devices. For instance, an IoT-driven real-time analytics system in a smart city could use DIDs to authenticate traffic sensors and ensure that only trusted devices contribute data to the pipeline. This reduces the risk of data poisoning attacks, where malicious actors inject false information to disrupt decision-making.

In addition to securing data, blockchain can be used to enforce compliance with data privacy regulations. Smart contracts—self-executing programs stored on a blockchain—can automate compliance workflows, such as deleting user data after a specified retention period or ensuring that data is processed only in authorized regions. For example, a healthcare provider using real-time analytics might deploy a smart contract to automatically anonymize patient data after it is processed, ensuring compliance with GDPR or HIPAA requirements.

Despite its advantages, integrating blockchain into real-time analytics systems comes with challenges, such as scalability and latency. Traditional blockchains, like Bitcoin or Ethereum, can struggle to handle the high transaction volumes and low-latency requirements of real-time systems. To address these limitations, organizations can explore solutions such as private blockchains, which offer faster processing speeds and greater control over network participants. Layer 2 scaling solutions, like sidechains or state channels, can also improve blockchain performance, making it more suitable for real-time applications.

7.2 Securing Supply Chains with Real-Time Analytics

Supply chains, which rely heavily on real-time analytics for efficiency and visibility, are a prime target for cyberattacks. Securing these systems requires a comprehensive approach that combines robust analytics practices with advanced security measures.

Real-time analytics in supply chains often involves tracking inventory levels, shipment locations, and delivery times across multiple vendors and regions. This level of integration creates vulnerabilities, as a breach in one part of the supply chain can compromise the entire system. For instance, attackers might infiltrate a vendor's IoT devices to inject false data, disrupting inventory forecasts and causing delays.

To secure supply chains, organizations must implement **end-of-end encryption** for all data transmitted between components of the analytics pipeline. This ensures that sensitive information, such as shipment details or supplier contracts, cannot be intercepted or altered during transmission. For example, an organization tracking real-time inventory movements might encrypt GPS data to prevent attackers from misdirecting shipments.

Another key strategy is the use of **digital twins**, virtual replicas of physical supply chain assets and processes. Digital twins powered by real-time analytics provide a secure environment for monitoring operations and detecting anomalies. For instance, if a shipment deviates from its expected route, the digital twin can alert supply chain managers and suggest corrective actions. This proactive approach minimizes the impact of disruptions and ensures that the supply chain remains resilient.

Organizations should also conduct regular **third-party risk assessments** to evaluate the security practices of their suppliers and partners. These assessments can identify weak links in the supply chain, such as outdated software or inadequate access controls, and provide recommendations for improvement. For example, a manufacturer using real-time analytics to monitor production might assess the cybersecurity posture of its raw material suppliers, ensuring that their systems meet industry standards.

Securing real-time analytics systems is a multifaceted challenge that demands a combination of advanced technologies, robust practices, and a proactive mindset. By integrating threat intelligence, leveraging blockchain, and addressing vulnerabilities in IoT and supply chain environments, organizations can build resilient systems that safeguard data while enabling real-time insights. These strategies not only protect sensitive information but also enhance trust and transparency, ensuring that real-time analytics remains a valuable tool for decision-making.

CHAPTER 8
Integrating Machine Learning in Real-Time Analytics

Machine learning is revolutionizing real-time analytics by making it possible to uncover patterns, predict outcomes, and make decisions autonomously as data flows through systems. Unlike traditional analytics methods, machine learning thrives in environments with dynamic, high-volume data, where the complexity of relationships within the data requires advanced algorithms to derive actionable insights. The synergy between machine learning and real-time analytics unlocks a level of intelligence that empowers organizations to operate with greater precision, speed, and adaptability.

One of the most impactful applications of machine learning in real-time analytics is predictive modeling. By analyzing historical and real-time data, machine learning algorithms can forecast trends and outcomes with remarkable accuracy. For example, a telecommunications company might use machine learning to predict network congestion based on current usage patterns, enabling them to optimize bandwidth allocation and improve customer experience. Similarly, in healthcare, real-time models trained on patient vitals can predict potential health complications before they manifest, allowing medical professionals to intervene proactively.

The ability of machine learning to perform anomaly detection in real-time is another significant advancement. Traditional rule-based systems struggle to keep up with the evolving nature of threats and irregularities. Machine learning models, however, can continuously learn and adapt, identifying deviations from normal patterns in real time. For instance, in the financial industry, machine learning models are used to monitor transaction streams, flagging unusual activities such as duplicate charges or out-of-pattern spending that might indicate fraud. This ability to detect anomalies instantly reduces risks and enhances operational integrity.

Machine learning also plays a pivotal role in personalization, a critical aspect of industries like retail, e-commerce, and entertainment. Real-time analytics systems powered by machine learning can analyze user behavior as it happens, delivering personalized recommendations that resonate with individual preferences. A streaming service, for example, might suggest a playlist or movie based on a viewer's current choices and past consumption patterns. In retail, machine learning can recommend products that complement a shopper's current cart, increasing the likelihood of cross-sell opportunities and boosting revenue.

Integrating machine learning into real-time analytics systems requires robust architectures capable of handling both the computational demands of machine learning models and the speed requirements of real-time data processing. The data pipeline must be designed to ingest, preprocess, and analyze data efficiently. This often involves deploying models in inference engines capable of making predictions with minimal latency. To achieve this, organizations commonly use specialized tools and frameworks, such as TensorFlow Serving or PyTorch Serve, which optimize models for real-time environments. Cloud platforms also play a crucial role, offering scalable resources for training and deploying models while ensuring they can process vast amounts of data in real time.

However, deploying machine learning in real-time analytics comes with its challenges. Ensuring the quality of incoming data is paramount, as real-time systems often deal with incomplete, noisy, or inconsistent data. Poor data quality can lead to inaccurate predictions and unreliable insights. To address this, organizations implement automated data validation and preprocessing techniques to clean and normalize data before it enters the pipeline. Another challenge is managing the computational complexity of machine learning models, especially those based on deep learning. These models require significant processing power, which can be a constraint in time-sensitive applications. Techniques such as model compression, pruning, and optimization are often employed to balance computational efficiency with accuracy.

Ethical considerations are also critical when integrating machine learning into real-time analytics. Models must be designed and trained to operate without bias, as biased outcomes can have far-reaching consequences, especially in sensitive areas such as hiring, lending, or law enforcement. For example, an algorithm used in real-time credit approvals must ensure fairness by avoiding biases that could unfairly disadvantage specific groups. Transparency in machine learning models is equally important, as decision-makers need to understand the reasoning behind model outputs to ensure accountability and trust.

Machine learning in real-time analytics is not just a tool for improving decision-making but a driver of innovation across industries. In manufacturing, predictive maintenance powered by machine learning allows companies to monitor equipment in real time, predicting failures before they occur and minimizing downtime. In transportation, real-time route optimization using machine learning enhances efficiency by considering variables such as traffic conditions, weather, and delivery schedules. These applications demonstrate the transformative potential of machine learning to reimagine traditional processes and deliver significant operational benefits.

The integration of machine learning into real-time analytics represents a paradigm shift in how organizations interact with data and make decisions. By enabling predictive capabilities, anomaly detection, and personalization, machine learning enhances the speed, accuracy, and intelligence of real-time systems. However, achieving these benefits requires a thoughtful approach to system design, data management, and ethical considerations.

The transformative potential of machine learning in real-time analytics extends beyond individual applications to redefine entire operational frameworks. It introduces an era where systems not only react to events as they occur but also anticipate future developments, dynamically adjusting strategies and actions in response to changing conditions. This capability to combine real-time responsiveness with foresight positions machine learning at the heart of modern analytics.

A significant advantage of machine learning in real-time analytics is its capacity for continuous learning. Unlike static algorithms that require manual updates, machine learning models evolve as they are exposed to new data. This adaptability ensures that predictions and recommendations remain relevant even as trends, behaviors, or environments change. For instance, in retail, machine learning models can adjust pricing strategies in real time based on fluctuations in demand, competitor actions, and inventory levels. This ensures that businesses remain competitive while optimizing revenue and customer satisfaction.

The role of reinforcement learning, a subset of machine learning, is gaining prominence in real-time analytics. Reinforcement learning allows models to make decisions and refine their strategies based on feedback from their environment. For example, in autonomous driving systems, reinforcement learning enables vehicles to continuously improve their navigation and safety decisions based on real-time interactions with their surroundings. Similarly, in energy management, reinforcement learning helps optimize the distribution of electricity across grids, balancing supply and demand dynamically while minimizing energy waste.

Another compelling application of machine learning in real-time analytics lies in its ability to process unstructured data, such as images, videos, and text, alongside structured data. This capability opens new possibilities for industries where traditional analytics have struggled to make sense of complex data types. In healthcare, real-time image recognition models can analyze diagnostic scans as they are generated, identifying abnormalities with speed and precision. In social media, natural language processing (NLP) models can analyze sentiment and trends in real time, enabling brands to respond promptly to customer feedback or emerging crises.

Machine learning also enhances decision-making in environments where stakes are high, and time is critical. In financial markets, for instance, algorithmic trading powered by real-time machine learning can execute trades in milliseconds based on live market conditions, maximizing profits while minimizing risks. Similarly, in cybersecurity, real-time models detect and neutralize threats such as malware, phishing attempts, or unauthorized access, protecting systems and sensitive data from harm. These applications demonstrate the ability of machine learning to empower organizations to act decisively and effectively in high-pressure scenarios.

The scalability of machine learning models is another factor driving their adoption in real-time analytics. Cloud platforms provide the infrastructure needed to train, deploy, and scale models across global operations. This scalability ensures that even organizations with extensive data volumes and geographically dispersed systems can benefit from machine learning. For example, an international logistics company might use real-time machine learning to optimize delivery routes across multiple regions simultaneously, adapting to local traffic patterns, weather conditions, and customer requirements.

However, the integration of machine learning into real-time analytics is not without its challenges. One of the most pressing is the need for interpretability. As machine learning models become more complex, understanding how they arrive at specific predictions or recommendations can become opaque, a phenomenon often referred to as the "black box" problem. For organizations operating in regulated industries, where transparency and accountability are paramount, this lack of interpretability can hinder adoption. To address this, explainable AI (XAI) techniques are being developed to provide insights into model decision-making processes, ensuring that outputs are both accurate and understandable.

Another challenge is the computational demand associated with real-time machine learning. Deep learning models, in particular, require significant resources for both training and inference. Organizations must strike a balance between performance and efficiency, leveraging techniques such as model optimization, edge computing, and hybrid architectures to meet their needs. For instance, a smart factory might use lightweight models at the edge to monitor equipment in real time, while leveraging more complex models in the cloud for long-term analysis and strategy development.

Data privacy and security remain critical concerns when deploying machine learning in real-time analytics. Organizations must ensure that sensitive data used to train and operate models is protected from unauthorized access and breaches. Federated learning is emerging as a solution to this challenge, enabling models to be trained across decentralized devices without requiring raw data to leave its source. For example, a healthcare organization using real-time machine learning to analyze patient data might employ federated learning to ensure compliance with privacy regulations while maintaining the accuracy of its models.

8.1 Autonomous Systems and Real-Time Decision-Making

The fusion of machine learning and real-time analytics has ushered in an era where systems not only react to data but also actively generate intelligence that anticipates and adapts to dynamic environments. One of the most ambitious frontiers of this integration is autonomous systems, which leverage real-time machine learning to make decisions independently, without human intervention. Autonomous vehicles are a prime example, relying on machine learning models to process massive amounts of sensory data in real time. These systems analyze inputs from cameras, radar, and GPS to detect objects on the road, predict the behavior of other drivers, and navigate safely. The challenge lies in ensuring these models operate with precision and reliability, as even minor errors can have significant consequences.

In manufacturing, autonomous robots equipped with real-time machine learning optimize production lines, detect faults, and adapt to changing demands seamlessly. For example, a robotic arm assembling electronics might use computer vision models to identify defective components before installation, improving product quality and reducing waste. By continuously learning from operational data, these robots refine their processes over time, enhancing efficiency and minimizing human intervention.

8.2 Multi-Modal Data Integration and Broader Applications

Another transformative area of real-time machine learning is multi-modal data integration, where data from diverse formats and sources is combined to generate more comprehensive insights. Many real-time systems have historically treated data in silos—categorizing it into text, images, or numerical data. Multi-modal machine learning breaks down these barriers, enabling systems to analyze and act on data holistically. For example, smart cities can integrate video surveillance, traffic sensors, and social media data in real time to monitor urban activity, predict traffic congestion, and allocate resources efficiently.

Healthcare is also benefiting from multi-modal machine learning, which provides a more holistic view of patients. Real-time systems can simultaneously analyze electronic health records, diagnostic images, and live vital signs to assist physicians in making more informed decisions. For instance, in an intensive care unit, a system might detect anomalies in scans while monitoring heart rate and oxygen levels, flagging potential complications for immediate intervention.

The scalability of real-time machine learning systems presents another critical opportunity. Global organizations, such as international retailers or logistics providers, must process real-time data across multiple time zones, cultures, and regulatory environments. This introduces challenges in localizing machine learning models to accommodate regional differences in preferences, languages, and trends. For example, a retailer's recommendation system must adapt to cultural nuances while delivering personalized suggestions to customers worldwide.

Finally, ethical considerations and energy efficiency are becoming essential focuses in the deployment of machine learning systems. Bias in machine learning models can have far-reaching implications in areas like hiring, credit scoring, and criminal justice. Organizations must prioritize fairness, transparency, and accountability by implementing robust governance policies. Simultaneously, as sustainability becomes a global priority, optimizing the energy consumption of machine learning workflows is critical. Techniques like model distillation, edge processing, and energy-aware training are helping organizations reduce their carbon footprints without compromising system performance.

In conclusion, the integration of machine learning into real-time analytics continues to push boundaries, enabling autonomy in machines and advancing multi-modal data integration for richer insights. However, challenges in scalability, ethics, and sustainability must be addressed to ensure these systems are deployed responsibly and effectively. By navigating these complexities, organizations can unlock limitless possibilities for innovation and value creation.

CHAPTER 9
Measuring and Maximizing the ROI of Real Time Analytics

Real-time analytics has transformed how organizations operate, offering the ability to process data instantaneously and make informed decisions on the fly. However, the effectiveness of these systems lies not only in their technical capabilities but also in their ability to deliver measurable value. This chapter explores strategies for evaluating the return on investment (ROI) of real-time analytics systems and maximizing their impact to ensure long-term success.

The ROI of real-time analytics can be assessed by examining both tangible and intangible benefits. Tangible benefits include increased revenue, cost savings, and operational efficiencies, while intangible benefits might encompass enhanced customer satisfaction, improved decision-making, and competitive advantage. To measure these benefits effectively, organizations must align their real-time analytics initiatives with specific business objectives. For instance, a retailer implementing a real-time recommendation engine might track metrics such as conversion rates, average order values, and customer retention to evaluate its impact.

One of the first steps in measuring ROI is establishing clear performance indicators that align with organizational goals. These key performance indicators (KPIs) should be specific, measurable, achievable, relevant, and time-bound (SMART). For example, a logistics company deploying real-time analytics to optimize delivery routes might define KPIs such as average delivery time, fuel consumption, and on-time delivery rates. By continuously monitoring these metrics, the company can gauge the system's effectiveness and identify areas for improvement.

Another crucial factor in measuring ROI is understanding the cost structure of real-time analytics systems. Costs can be broadly categorized into initial setup expenses, operational costs, and scalability costs. Initial setup expenses include investments in infrastructure, software, and system integration. Operational costs encompass expenses related to data storage, processing, and maintenance, while scalability costs arise from expanding the system to handle increased data volumes or additional use cases. By tracking these costs against the benefits delivered, organizations can determine whether their real-time analytics investments are yielding positive returns.

Maximizing the ROI of real-time analytics requires more than just cost-benefit analysis involves optimizing system performance and ensuring that insights are translated into actionable outcomes. One way to achieve this is by fostering a culture of data-driven decision-making across the organization. Employees at all levels must be empowered to leverage real-time insights into their workflows, whether it's a sales team responding to customer trends or a manufacturing unit adjusting production schedules. Providing training and tools for data literacy ensures that employees can interpret and act on insights effectively, amplifying the value of real-time analytics.

Automation is another key strategy for maximizing ROI. By automating routine tasks and decision-making processes, organizations can reduce manual effort, minimize errors, and improve efficiency. For example, in the finance sector, real-time analytics systems can automate fraud detection by flagging suspicious transactions for further review, freeing up analysts to focus on higher-value activities. Similarly, in e-commerce, automated inventory management systems powered by real-time analytics can adjust stock levels dynamically based on demand forecasts, reducing the risk of overstocking or stockouts.

Personalization is a powerful driver of ROI in customer-facing applications of real-time analytics. By tailoring products, services, and experiences to individual preferences, organizations can enhance customer engagement and loyalty. For instance, a streaming platform using real-time analytics might personalize content recommendations for each user, increasing watch time and reducing churn. Personalization not only boosts immediate revenue but also strengthens long-term customer relationships, creating a sustainable competitive advantage.

Scalability is another critical aspect of maximizing ROI. As organizations grow and their data volumes increase, real-time analytics systems must scale efficiently to handle new demands. Cloud platforms provide the flexibility needed to scale resources dynamically, ensuring that systems remain cost-effective as they expand. For example, an online retailer experiencing a surge in traffic during a holiday season can scale its recommendation engine to handle the increased load, ensuring a seamless customer experience while capitalizing on peak demand.

Innovation and continuous improvement are essential for sustaining the ROI of real-time analytics over time. Organizations must regularly review and refine their systems to incorporate new technologies, address emerging challenges, and seize new opportunities. For instance, incorporating machine learning into real-time analytics systems can enhance predictive capabilities, enabling organizations to anticipate customer needs, optimize operations, and drive growth. Additionally, integrating emerging technologies like edge computing or blockchain can further enhance the efficiency, security, and scalability of real-time analytics systems.

Finally, collaboration and partnerships play a vital role in maximizing the value of real-time analytics. By working with technology providers, consultants, and academic institutions, organizations can access expertise, tools, and resources that accelerate innovation and drive better outcomes. For example, a healthcare provider implementing real-time patient monitoring might partner with a technology company to develop advanced analytics models, ensuring that the system delivers accurate and actionable insights.

Measuring and maximizing the ROI of real-time analytics requires a comprehensive approach that combines clear goal setting, performance monitoring, and strategic optimization. By aligning analytics initiatives with business objectives, fostering a data-driven culture, and leveraging automation and personalization, organizations can unlock the full potential of real-time systems. Additionally, continuous innovation, scalability, and collaboration ensure that these systems remain valuable assets in an ever-changing landscape. As organizations refine their approaches to real-time analytics, they not only improve their bottom lines but also enhance their ability to adapt, compete, and thrive in the future.

To truly maximize the ROI of real-time analytics, organizations must go beyond traditional performance tracking and delve into the strategic integration of insights across all operational layers. Real-time analytics is not merely a tool for data processing; it is a framework for transformation. By embedding its capabilities into core business strategies and decision-making processes, organizations can unlock exponential value that extends far beyond immediate gains.

A critical element of this integration is the alignment of real-time analytics with long-term strategic goals. Organizations must view these systems not as isolated projects but as foundational enablers of growth, innovation, and resilience. For instance, a supply chain company could integrate real-time analytics into its strategic vision for end-to-end visibility, leveraging insights to optimize inventory, reduce waste, and enhance supplier relationships. By embedding real-time analytics into their vision for sustainability, companies can simultaneously achieve cost savings and improve environmental outcomes, creating a dual-layered return on investment.

Another dimension of maximizing value lies in the cross-functional application of real-time analytics insights. When different departments—marketing, operations, finance, and customer service have access to shared, synchronized real-time data, the organization as a whole can act cohesively and make informed, unified decisions. For example, marketing teams can adjust campaigns based on live customer sentiment data, while operations teams can ensure inventory levels align with promotional activities. This cross-functional synergy not only drives efficiency but also enhances the overall customer experience, creating a virtuous cycle of value creation.

To sustain the ROI of real-time analytics, organizations must also prioritize adaptability and responsiveness to market trends. Markets are dynamic, and the competitive landscape can shift rapidly. Real-time analytics allows businesses to stay ahead by identifying emerging trends as they unfold. For example, in retail, a company might use real-time sales data to detect surges in demand for specific products, enabling them to pivot their marketing, supply chain, and inventory strategies accordingly. This agility can spell the difference between seizing an opportunity and falling behind competitors.

One often-overlooked aspect of maximizing ROI is leveraging real-time analytics to drive innovation. By analyzing patterns and anomalies in real-time data, organizations can uncover unmet needs, inefficiencies, and untapped opportunities. For instance, a telecommunications company might use real-time network usage data to identify underserved regions, informing decisions about infrastructure investments. Similarly, in product development, real-time customer feedback can guide iterative improvements, ensuring that new offerings are aligned with market demand.

Furthermore, organizations must adopt a forward-looking approach to ROI by investing in the scalability and future proofing of their real-time analytics systems. As data volumes grow and use cases expand, these systems must be capable of evolving without significant disruptions or cost escalations. Cloud-based architectures, modular designs, and the adoption of emerging technologies such as edge computing and serverless frameworks provide the flexibility needed to accommodate future demands. For example, a healthcare provider might implement a scalable real-time patient monitoring system that can easily integrate new devices or data streams as medical technologies advance.

Finally, organizations must recognize the value of customer trust and satisfaction as intangible yet essential components of ROI. Real-time analytics systems often process sensitive customer data and ensuring that this data is handled securely and ethically is paramount. Transparent communication about how data is collected, analyzed, and used fosters trust and builds stronger customer relationships. For instance, an e-commerce platform using real-time recommendation systems can assure customers that their data is being used to improve their shopping experience rather than for intrusive or unauthorized purposes. This trust translates into loyalty, repeat business, and positive brand reputation, key drivers of long-term ROI.

The true ROI of real-time analytics is realized when these systems are seamlessly integrated into the fabric of an organization, driving strategic alignment, cross-functional synergy, innovation, and adaptability. By maintaining a focus on scalability, ethical practices, and customer-centricity, organizations can amplify the value of their investments and position themselves for sustained success in an increasingly data-driven world. As we transition to the final chapter, the focus will shift to envisioning the future of real-time analytics, exploring the trends, technologies, and paradigms that will shape its evolution and unlock new opportunities for innovation.

9.1 Building a Feedback Loop for Continuous Optimization

One often underutilized approach to maximizing the ROI of real-time analytics is establishing a feedback loop that ensures the system improves over time. Feedback loops are instrumental in aligning real-time analytics systems with evolving business objectives, customer needs, and market dynamics. By feeding the insights generated by these systems back into their processes, organizations can iteratively refine their operations and strategies.

For instance, a retail business leveraging real-time analytics for personalized marketing campaigns could track customer engagement metrics, such as click-through rates and conversion rates, to assess the effectiveness of its efforts. This data can then be used to adjust recommendation algorithms, optimize promotional strategies, or refine audience segmentation. Similarly, in manufacturing, a feedback loop might involve monitoring the performance of predictive maintenance models and fine-tuning them based on observed equipment behavior and failure rates, ensuring greater accuracy and reliability over time.

To implement an effective feedback loop, organizations must establish clear mechanisms for collecting performance metrics, analyzing outcomes, and making adjustments. Automated tools and dashboards play a critical role in this process, providing stakeholders with real-time visibility into system performance and actionable insights for improvement. Furthermore, organizations must foster a culture of learning and adaptation, encouraging teams to experiment, iterate, and embrace continuous improvement.

9.2 Monetizing Real-Time Analytics Insights

Another way to maximize the ROI of real-time analytics is to explore opportunities for monetizing the insights these systems generate. Organizations that successfully harness real-time analytics can often identify valuable data and intelligence that can be leveraged to create new revenue streams or enhance existing offerings.

In many industries, aggregated and anonymized data from real-time analytics systems can be packaged and sold as a standalone product or service. For example, a logistics company that uses real-time data to optimize delivery routes might monetize its traffic patterns and delivery performance insights by offering them to urban planners, transportation agencies, or retailers. Similarly, a telecommunications company could provide network usage analytics to advertisers or content providers seeking to optimize their offerings for specific demographics or geographies.

Real-time analytics also opens the door to new business models based on subscription or pay-per-use services. For instance, an energy provider using real-time analytics to manage grid performance might offer dynamic pricing plans that adjust rates based on real-time demand and supply conditions, benefiting both the company and its customers. These innovative models not only generate revenue but also differentiate the organization from competitors, enhancing its market position.

Additionally, organizations can monetize their real-time analytics capabilities by offering them as a service to other businesses. Platforms like Amazon Web Services (AWS) and Microsoft Azure have built thriving businesses by providing scalable real-time analytics tools and infrastructure to companies across industries. Smaller organizations can emulate this model by creating niche solutions tailored to specific sectors or use cases, such as real-time customer sentiment analysis for retail or live network monitoring for telecommunications.

Monetization strategies must be pursued with care to ensure that they align with organizational values and customer expectations. Transparency and data privacy are paramount, and any initiative involving the sale or sharing of analytics insights must comply with relevant regulations and ethical standards. Customers should be informed about how their data is used, and safeguards must be in place to protect sensitive information.

Maximizing the ROI of real-time analytics goes beyond measuring immediate financial returns, it involves creating systems that continuously learn, adapt, and evolve to deliver sustained value. By establishing feedback loops for optimization, leveraging insights for monetization, and aligning analytics systems with strategic goals, organizations can unlock the full potential of their real-time capabilities. These efforts not only drive operational efficiencies and revenue growth but also position organizations as leaders in innovation, adaptability, and customer-centricity.

CHAPTER 10
Envisioning the Future of Real-Time Analytics

The future of real-time analytics is one of unprecedented potential, where emerging technologies, evolving business needs, and societal shifts converge to create transformative opportunities. As data continues to grow in volume, velocity, and variety, the role of real-time analytics will expand from being a tool for decision-making to becoming the backbone of intelligent, adaptive systems that drive innovation and resilience. This chapter explores the trends, technologies, and paradigms that will shape the future of real-time analytics, unlocking new frontiers for growth and impact.

One of the most significant trends shaping real-time analytics is the rise of **ubiquitous computing**. With the proliferation of IoT devices, edge computing, and 5G connectivity, data generation is becoming more decentralized and pervasive. Real-time analytics will increasingly operate at the edge, processing data closer to its source to reduce latency, improve responsiveness, and minimize bandwidth usage. For example, in smart cities, edge-based real-time analytics systems will analyze traffic patterns, air quality, and energy consumption at the neighborhood level, enabling hyper-localized interventions that improve urban living conditions. Similarly, in healthcare, wearable devices will deliver real-time insights about patient health directly to providers, facilitating faster diagnoses and more personalized care.

The integration of **artificial intelligence (AI)** and **machine learning (ML)** will further elevate the capabilities of real-time analytics. AI-powered systems will move beyond reactive analysis to proactive and even autonomous decision-making. For instance, predictive maintenance systems in manufacturing will not only anticipate equipment failures but also autonomously order replacement parts and schedule repairs. In retail, AI-driven real-time analytics will create hyper-personalized customer experiences, dynamically adjusting offers, prices, and recommendations based on individual behavior and context. These advancements will enable organizations to operate with greater efficiency, agility, and precision.

Another key development is the growing importance of **real-time analytics in sustainability and environmental stewardship**. As organizations and governments strive to meet ambitious climate goals, real-time systems will play a crucial role in monitoring and managing environmental impact. For example, energy companies will use real-time analytics to optimize the integration of renewable energy sources into the grid, balancing supply, and demand dynamically. Similarly, agricultural operations will rely on real-time insights to reduce water usage, minimize chemical inputs, and improve crop yields. By enabling data-driven sustainability practices, real-time analytics will become a cornerstone of global efforts to combat climate change and preserve natural resources.

The future of real-time analytics also lies in its ability to facilitate **collaborative intelligence**, where humans and machines work together to solve complex problems. Real-time dashboards and decision-support systems will provide actionable insights while empowering human users to apply their intuition, creativity, and expertise. For example, in disaster response, real-time analytics systems will analyze satellite imagery, weather data, and social media feeds to identify affected areas and prioritize resources. These insights will guide responders in making life-saving decisions, demonstrating the power of human-machine collaboration.

The ethical implications of real-time analytics will also take center stage in the coming years. As these systems become more pervasive, questions around data privacy, fairness, and accountability will grow in importance. Organizations must adopt robust governance frameworks to ensure that real-time analytics systems operate transparently and ethically. This includes implementing safeguards to protect user data, addressing biases in machine learning models, and providing clear explanations for automated decisions. By prioritizing ethical considerations, organizations can build trust with stakeholders and ensure that real-time analytics serves as a force for good.

The democratization of real-time analytics is another trend that will shape its future. Advances in user-friendly tools and interfaces will make it easier for non-technical users to harness the power of real-time data. This democratization will empower employees across all levels of an organization to make data-driven decisions, fostering a culture of innovation and collaboration. For instance, sales representatives might use real-time analytics to tailor their pitches during client meetings, while HR teams could monitor employee engagement in real time to address potential issues proactively.

As real-time analytics evolves, it will also intersect with **emerging technologies** like quantum computing and blockchain. Quantum computing has the potential to revolutionize real-time analytics by solving complex optimization problems and processing massive datasets at unprecedented speeds. For example, quantum algorithms could enable real-time traffic optimization across entire cities, reducing congestion and emissions. Blockchain, on the other hand, will enhance the security and integrity of real-time systems by providing tamper-proof audit trails and enabling decentralized data sharing. These technologies will expand the possibilities for real-time analytics, opening new avenues for innovation and efficiency.

In addition to technological advancements, the **economic and societal impacts of real-time analytics** will become increasingly apparent. Industries such as healthcare, education, and public safety will benefit from the transformative power of real-time insights, improving outcomes and enhancing quality of life. For example, real-time analytics in education could provide personalized learning experiences for students, adapting content and pacing based on individual progress. In public safety, real-time crime analytics could help law enforcement agencies allocate resources more effectively, preventing incidents before they occur.

Finally, the future of real-time analytics will be shaped by the growing emphasis on **resilience and adaptability**. In an era of rapid change and uncertainty, organizations will rely on real-time systems to navigate disruptions, seize opportunities, and maintain competitive advantage. Whether responding to supply chain disruptions, adapting to shifting consumer preferences, or managing public health crises, real-time analytics will provide the agility needed to thrive in an unpredictable world.

The future of real-time analytics is one of boundless potential, driven by advancements in technology, a focus on sustainability, and a commitment to ethical practices. As organizations embrace ubiquitous computing, AI integration, and collaborative intelligence, they will unlock new opportunities for innovation, efficiency, and impact. By addressing challenges such as data privacy, democratization, and resilience, real-time analytics will continue to shape the future, enabling organizations and societies to thrive in a data-driven era. The journey ahead is not just about harnessing data but about leveraging it to build a smarter, more sustainable, and equitable world.

The future of real-time analytics is poised to be even more transformative as it becomes deeply ingrained in everyday systems and decision-making processes. This evolution will be fueled by advancements that push the boundaries of what real-time analytics can achieve, extending their reach to virtually every aspect of human activity and industry operations. However, to fully realize its potential, the continued development of infrastructure, governance, and innovation ecosystems will be essential.

One area that remains ripe for exploration is **hyper-personalization at scale**, where real-time analytics intersects with granular user insights to create individualized experiences for millions simultaneously. Hyper-personalization will redefine customer interactions by leveraging live data from multiple touchpoints—mobile devices, wearables, social platforms, and IoT-connected environments. For example, in the hospitality industry, real-time analytics can curate personalized travel experiences by analyzing a traveler's past bookings, preferences, and live feedback. Hotels can adjust in-room amenities, dining suggestions, and entertainment options based on real-time guest behavior. The challenge will be maintaining this level of personalization without compromising user privacy, necessitating stronger data governance frameworks and transparent policies.

Real-time autonomous decision-making will also emerge as a major trend. While machine learning models and AI are already driving autonomy in systems such as self-driving cars and industrial robots, the next stage will involve systems operating collaboratively across networks. Imagine autonomous supply chains where factories, warehouses, and logistics providers interact in real time to manage inventory, allocate resources, and reroute shipments—all without human intervention. Such interconnected systems will rely on real-time analytics to process massive datasets from distributed nodes and adjust actions dynamically to meet changing conditions. This level of autonomy has the potential to revolutionize efficiency and productivity, but it also introduces complexities in terms of system coordination, error management, and accountability.

Another promising development is **real-time simulation and digital twins**, which enable organizations to model and test scenarios in live environments. A digital twin is a virtual replica of a physical asset, system, or process that is continuously updated with real-time data. These models allow for dynamic simulations that can predict outcomes, identify inefficiencies, and recommend interventions. For instance, in urban planning, a city could use digital twins of its infrastructure to test the impact of new traffic regulations or construction projects, optimizing outcomes before implementation. In healthcare, digital twins of patients, built using real-time data from wearable devices and medical records, could help doctors predict how individuals might respond to treatments, personalizing care at an unprecedented level.

The growing integration of **human-centric design in real-time systems** will further enhance their usability and adoption. Real-time analytics will become more intuitive and accessible, empowering even non-technical users to interact with and benefit from live insights. Advances in natural language processing (NLP) will enable conversational interfaces where users can ask questions and receive actionable insights in plain language. For example, a marketing manager might ask, "Which product is trending in the Southeast region right now?" and receive a real-time visualization along with recommendations for next steps. This shift toward simplicity and inclusivity will democratize analytics, driving innovation across industries by putting the power of data into the hands of more people.

The **role of real-time analytics in crisis management** will also expand as organizations and governments prepare for increasingly unpredictable global challenges. Whether responding to natural disasters, pandemics, or geopolitical events, real-time analytics will provide critical insights for rapid decision-making. During a hurricane, for instance, emergency management agencies could use live data from weather sensors, transportation networks, and social media to predict affected areas, optimize evacuation routes, and deploy resources effectively. Similarly, in the face of public health crises, real-time analytics could track disease spread, monitor hospital capacities, and coordinate vaccination efforts, saving lives and reducing societal disruptions.

As these systems become more powerful and interconnected, **governance and regulation** will play a pivotal role in ensuring their responsible use. Governments and international bodies must work collaboratively to establish frameworks that address data privacy, security, and ethical considerations. For instance, global standards for data sharing and interoperability will be necessary to facilitate cross-border applications of real-time analytics, such as in international trade or global health initiatives. At the same time, organizations will need to build internal governance structures to ensure that their real-time analytics systems align with ethical principles, regulatory requirements, and stakeholder expectations.

Sustainability will remain a central theme as organizations adopt real-time analytics to meet environmental and social goals. By integrating real-time systems into sustainability initiatives, businesses can track and reduce their carbon footprints, optimize resource usage, and improve transparency in supply chains. For example, retailers might use real-time analytics to monitor the environmental impact of their logistics operations, identifying opportunities to switch to greener transportation methods or reduce packaging waste. Beyond corporate applications, real-time systems will play a vital role in addressing broader challenges like deforestation, water scarcity, and energy transition, leveraging live data to inform policies and drive collective action.

Finally, the emergence of **quantum-powered real-time analytics** will redefine the scale and speed of data processing. Quantum computing has the potential to handle complex, multidimensional problems that traditional systems struggle to solve, such as optimizing global transportation networks or modeling climate systems in real time. While quantum computing is still in its early stages, its integration with real-time analytics could unlock capabilities that seem unimaginable today, propelling industries into entirely new paradigms.

10.1 The Role of Interconnectivity in the Future of Real-Time Analytics

One area that has not been fully explored is the increasing importance of interconnectivity among systems, organizations, and industries in the evolution of real-time analytics. As data ecosystems become more integrated, real-time analytics will no longer operate in isolated silos but as part of a vast, interconnected network were data flows seamlessly across systems and entities. This shift will enable unprecedented levels of collaboration, innovation, and efficiency.

For instance, in global supply chains, interconnected real-time analytics systems can facilitate end-to-end visibility, allowing manufacturers, distributors, and retailers to share live updates on inventory levels, shipping statuses, and demand fluctuations. This transparency reduces inefficiencies, mitigates disruptions, and ensures that resources are allocated optimally across the value chain. Similarly, in healthcare, interconnected real-time systems can enable hospitals, clinics, and public health agencies to share anonymized patient data, improving disease surveillance, resource allocation, and collaborative treatment efforts.

The interconnectivity of real-time analytics will also play a critical role in tackling global challenges like climate change. By linking data from disparate sources—such as satellite imagery, IoT-enabled sensors, and governmental reports—real-time analytics systems can provide a comprehensive view of environmental conditions and facilitate coordinated responses. For example, a network of real-time systems could monitor deforestation activities across multiple countries, alerting authorities to illegal logging while enabling reforestation initiatives to target the most impacted areas. This level of collaboration would not be possible without the seamless exchange of data powered by interconnectivity.

However, with greater interconnectivity comes the challenge of ensuring data interoperability, security, and privacy. Standardizing data formats and communication protocols will be essential to enable different systems to interact effectively. Organizations must also invest in secure data-sharing frameworks that protect sensitive information while fostering trust among collaborators. For example, blockchain technology can be used to maintain tamper-proof records of data exchanges, ensuring transparency and accountability in interconnected ecosystems.

10.2 Human-Centered Real-Time Analytics: The Next Frontier

As real-time analytics systems become more advanced and pervasive, their design and implementation must increasingly prioritize human needs and experiences. Human-centered real-time analytics focuses on creating systems that enhance, rather than replace, human decision-making, fostering collaboration, accessibility, and inclusivity.

One aspect of human-centered analytics is designing intuitive interfaces that make insights accessible to non-technical users. While real-time analytics has traditionally been the domain of data scientists and analysts, advancements in natural language processing (NLP) and conversational AI are making it possible for anyone to interact with these systems effortlessly. For instance, a small business owner could ask a voice-enabled analytics tool, "What's causing the dip in sales this week?" and receive a clear, actionable explanation, complete with visualizations, within seconds. By lowering the barriers to entry, human-centered analytics democratizes access to real-time insights, enabling more individuals and organizations to benefit.

Another critical focus of human-centered real-time analytics is fostering collaboration between humans and machines. Instead of relying solely on automated decision-making, future systems will prioritize hybrid approaches where humans and AI work together to achieve better outcomes. For example, in emergency response scenarios, a real-time analytics system might provide responders with live data on the location and severity of an incident while leaving critical judgment calls such as prioritizing rescue efforts to human operators. This synergy combines the speed and precision of machines with the empathy and contextual understanding of humans.

Inclusivity will also be a cornerstone of human-centered real-time analytics, ensuring that systems cater to diverse users across geographies, languages, and abilities. For example, in regions with limited internet connectivity, lightweight, offline-capable analytics tools can enable local businesses and communities to leverage real-time insights. Similarly, incorporating accessibility features such as screen readers, adjustable text sizes, and multilingual support—ensures that these systems are usable by individuals with disabilities or those who speak less commonly supported languages.

The ethical implications of human-centered real-time analytics cannot be overlooked. As these systems become integral to decision-making processes, they must be designed to respect user privacy, prevent bias, and maintain transparency. For instance, an AI-powered hiring platform using real-time analytics must ensure that its recommendations are free from biases that could disadvantage certain demographic groups. Similarly, organizations deploying customer-facing analytics tools should clearly communicate how user data is collected and used, fostering trust and confidence in their systems.

As real-time analytics continues to evolve, its future will be defined by interconnectivity and a focus on human-centered design. The ability to link systems, organizations, and industries through interconnected real-time analytics will unlock new opportunities for collaboration and innovation, addressing challenges that require collective action and shared insights. At the same time, prioritizing human needs in the design and implementation of these systems will ensure that real-time analytics enhances decision-making, fosters inclusivity, and respects ethical principles.

www.ingramcontent.com/pod-product-compliance
Lightning Source LLC
LaVergne TN
LVHW092008090526
838202LV00001B/46